THE
WOODWIND PLAYER'S
COOKBOOK
Creative Recipes
for a Successful Performance

Published by
Meredith Music Publications
a division of G.W. Music, Inc.
4899 Lerch Creek Ct., Galesville, MD 20765
http://www.meredithmusic.com

MEREDITH MUSIC PUBLICATIONS and its stylized double M logo are trademarks of
MEREDITH MUSIC PUBLICATIONS, a division of G.W. Music, Inc.

International Standard Book Number: 978-1-57463-097-8
Library of Congress Control Number: 2008922492
Printed and bound in U.S.A.

Contents

Foreword

An eclectic collection of authors if there ever was one! Surely this volume's readership will be the same. Will Rogers' statement that, "Even if you're on the right track, you'll get run over if you just sit there," might be an observation deeply understood by our readers, as it certainly is understood by our authors. The fact that you have picked up this book and have begun to read its recipes is strong indication that you're not only on the right track, but you, like they, are tremendously averse to being run over!

The job of project coordinator for *The Woodwind Player's Cookbook: Creative Recipes for a Successful Performance* was one of finding authors from all corners who have two things in common: (1) consummate personal success in some facet of a profession involving the woodwinds, and (2) a desire to improve woodwind playing and teaching overall by generously sharing some treasured bit of knowledge that they have acquired and honed through years of personal experience. Aside from these two factors, our authors are incredibly diverse, representing major symphony orchestras, more major universities and conservatories than I care to list, immensely successful private studios serving young and old alike, and some very interesting private practices, including that of a hand therapist and of a specialist in physical problems of performers. There are transcribers, editors, technicians, designers of tools, and makers of reeds. On the list of authors are Grammy Award winners, world-class performers and teachers, top military band performers, a public school teacher whose national "Teacher of the Year" awards speak volumes about his success, a longtime reed performer and road manager from the Glenn Miller Band, and highly successful freelancers whose resourcefulness and willingness to reinvent themselves constantly has brought them sustained success over a substantial time period. I hope that you will enjoy their viewpoints, their humor, their experience and their wisdom as this wonderful fraternity of accomplished professionals shares their passions with you.

Special thanks to all of the authors, who received no remuneration for their contributions. Also, a very special thanks to Mary Jo, without whose help this would not have happened.

Buon appetito!

Charles West
Project Director/Editor

Acknowledgments

To each of the *chefs* who contributed to this publication, I offer my sincere thanks. Each individual responded to our initial invitation with a resounding "yes." They were each enthusiastic about being involved in what they felt would be a unique and worthwhile contribution to woodwind playing and to music education. Their generosity has been exceptional, their expertise unquestionable, and their love of woodwind playing and music education inspiring. The writings within, presented by them, are based on years of study and experience from a variety of educational and professional levels.

Profound thanks and admiration are extended to Chuck West, editor and coordinator of this volume. Chuck could, and should, write a book on organization and management; his skills are incredible! He is a creative and talented individual to whom I owe a great deal of thanks for his tireless work on this project. Chuck went about the task of selecting authors, organizing and collecting materials, motivating writers, and editing text with energy and enthusiasm. In addition to being a superb musician, Chuck is also an educator of the highest order, which is apparent in the composition of this volume. Thanks to Chuck West, the world now has a collection of interesting and insightful articles contained in one volume, written by many of today's most outstanding woodwind players and pedagogues. To Shawn Girsberger my unending gratitude for her work with Meredith Music Publications and for the artistic layout and cover design of this volume. Sincere thanks are also expressed to Susan Gedutis-Lindsay for her sharp eye and insightful comments as proofreader/editor. For leading the way in support of music education in our schools and for their assistance in marketing, thanks to Joe Lamond, President and CEO of NAMM and the American Music Conference.

And finally, to the thousands of music students and their directors who have inspired each of us, our never-ending thanks for your dedication, beautiful music making, and the belief that music does make a difference.

Garwood Whaley
President and Founder
Meredith Music Publications

∾ ∾ ∾

About the Authors

Ann Adams teaches applied oboe, chamber music, and music education classes at Stetson University, where she has been since 1989. She received the B.M. degree from Western Michigan University and the M.M., M.M.E., and D.M. degrees from Florida State University.

Valarie Anderson has performed extensively in solo and chamber concerts in the US, Canada, Norway, Germany, and South America. She taught oboe at the University of Alberta and at Virginia Tech, and was principal oboist with the Roanoke (Virginia) Symphony. Widely recognized for her expertise in oboe reed-making equipment, she is the owner of Jeanné, Inc., and currently performs and develops new products for clarinetists and double reed performers.

Shelley Binder is Associate Professor of Music at the University of Tennessee. Dr. Binder attended North Carolina School for the Arts, the Cincinnati Conservatory, Virginia Commonwealth, and Florida State University, where she earned her D.M. She has played with the Virginia Symphony, Virginia Opera, and Central Wisconsin Symphony Orchestras. She has appeared as a recitalist and clinician throughout the United States. She is a student of Louis Moyse, and recently finished writing his biography.

J. Lawrie Bloom holds the position of Clarinet and Solo Bass Clarinet with the Chicago Symphony Orchestra, is the clarinetist with the Rembrandt Chamber Players, and is artistic codirector of the Eastern Shore Chamber Music Festival in Maryland. He is a Senior Lecturer in Clarinet at the Northwestern University School of Music and an artist/performer for Buffet Crampon, USA, and RICO International.

Leone Buyse is Joseph and Ida Kirkland Mullen Professor of Flute at Rice University's Shepherd School of Music in Houston. Formerly on the faculty of the University of Michigan, New England Conservatory, and Boston University, she served as a principal flutist of the Boston Symphony and Boston Pops, and as a member of the San Francisco Symphony and Rochester Philharmonic. She has presented recitals and master classes across the United States and in Canada, Europe, Japan, New Zealand, and Australia.

Mary Karen Clardy, Professor of Flute at University of North Texas, appears as soloist, chamber artist, and teacher throughout the United States, Canada, Mexico, Europe, Asia, and South America. A renowned author, current volumes include over ten books from European American Music, Leduc, Schott, and Universal Edition. Her students are consistent prizewinners in international competitions and occupy prominent orchestral and faculty positions throughout the world.

William J. Dawson, M.D. is Professor Emeritus of Orthopedic Surgery at Northwestern University and past-president of the Performing Arts Medicine Association. He is medical consultant to the International Double Reed Society and the Association of Concert Bands, and has authored more than one hundred twenty articles, books, and book chapters involving medical problems of instrumentalists, and has lectured internationally. A symphonic bassoonist for forty-five years, he also teaches bassoon privately in the Chicago suburbs.

Doris DeLoach is Professor of Oboe at Baylor University in Waco, Texas. She is active as a teacher and performer. Her teachers include Nancy Fowler at Florida State University (B.M. and D.M.), Ray Still, and John deLancie. She performs with the Baylor Woodwind Quintet and Waco Symphony Orchestra, and she has played throughout the United States as well as in France, Germany, Austria, the Netherlands, Costa Rica, and Panama. Her students have teaching and playing careers throughout the United States.

Julie DeRoche is Associate Professor of Clarinet and chair of Performance Studies at the DePaul University School of Music. She performs and tours regularly with the Chicago Symphony Orchestra, has served as president of the International Clarinet Association, and is an artist/clinician for the Leblanc Division of Conn-Selmer, Inc.

William Dietz, Professor of Bassoon and Wind Chamber Music, has been a faculty member at the University of Arizona since 1983. He is the senior author and editor of *Teaching Woodwinds*, a text designed for college wind instrumental techniques classes, and is a frequent contributor to professional journals.

Mike Duva plays woodwinds in the house band at the Alabama Theatre in North Myrtle Beach, South Carolina. After study at New Mexico State University and The University of North Texas, he spent eleven years as baritone saxophonist and road manager with the Glenn Miller Orchestra. His teachers include Charles West, John Scott, Jim Riggs, and Sam Trimble. His collaborations include the Temptations/Four Tops, Gladys Knight and the Pips, Johnny Mathis, Rosemary Clooney, Mel Torme, Bob Hope, Vic Damone, and albums with the Glenn Miller Orchestra and Barry Manilow.

Clark W Fobes received his M.M. from the San Francisco Conservatory in 1983. He performs regularly in the San Francisco Bay Area with the San Francisco Opera, Symphony, and Ballet orchestras, and the California Symphony. He often doubles, playing bass clarinet, contrabass clarinet, basset horn, or E-flat soprano clarinet. Clark W Fobes is recognized internationally as one of the leading makers of superior hand-finished mouthpieces and barrels for the clarinet.

Edward Fraedrich is a saxophonist and saxophone teacher in the Washington, DC area. He has been soloist with the National Symphony Orchestra, the Fairfax Symphony, the Capitol Wind Symphony, and many other organizations. He was the saxophone teacher at Virginia Commonwealth University for eleven years and now maintains a large private saxophone studio in Fairfax County, Virginia. Mr. Fraedrich's teachers include George Etheridge, Dale Underwood, and Donald Sinta, and he has recorded on the Klavier label.

Laurie Glencross is Associate Professor of Flute at Millikin University in Decatur, Illinois, where she plays principal flute in the Millikin-Decatur Symphony Orchestra and the Millikin Faculty Woodwind Quintet. She received both bachelor and master of music degrees from the Manhattan School of Music and completed a doctor of music degree from Florida State University.

Victor L. Goines is Professor of Music and Director of Jazz Studies at Northwestern University and formerly Artistic Director of Jazz Studies at the Juilliard School and a member of the Jazz at Lincoln Center Orchestra with Wynton Marsalis. He holds a bachelor of music education from Loyola University in New Orleans and a master of music from Virginia Commonwealth University.

Susan Goodfellow is Professor of Flute at the University of Utah. She holds degrees from Juilliard School of Music and the University of Chicago. She has performed with the New York City Symphony, the Chicago Chamber Orchestra, and the Utah Symphony, and has soloed with the Carmel Bach Festival and the Mormon Tabernacle Choir.

Bruce Hammel is Associate Professor of Music at Virginia Commonwealth University, where he serves as artist/teacher of bassoon, and teaches courses in music theory and aural skills. In addition to extensive performing and recording experience, he develops Web-based instructional materials for bassoon and theory. He holds his D.M. from Florida State University and other degrees from the University of Michigan, the SUNY Postdam, and Hamilton College.

Diana Haskell is assistant principal clarinet and E-flat clarinet with St. Louis Symphony Orchestra. She previously was assistant principal clarinet with the Milwaukee Symphony Orchestra, and has been principal clarinet with Santa Fe Opera, Buffalo Philharmonic, Savannah Symphony, and Charleston Symphony Orchestras. A graduate of Juilliard and Eastman, and she was a finalist in the 1985 Naumberg International Competition, resulting in a solo recital in Carnegie Hall. Her CD, *Clarinet Enchantments*, is available at www.aamrecordings.com or on *iTunes*.

Wayne Hedrick is a "world-class" instrumentalist, according to *Fanfare* magazine. He has an extensive discography of over seventy albums on numerous labels, including flute and harp recordings, solo flute and wind ensemble pieces, chamber music, wind ensemble recordings, studio recordings, and a Grammy-winner on the Telarc label. Wayne was the principal flutist of the USAF Heritage of America Band for over twenty years. He currently freelances in Virginia and lives with his wife and two daughters.

Rob Holmes has been playing saxophone professionally for more than twenty years. He has a bachelor's degree in jazz performance from the University of Miami, Florida and a master's degree in composition from Virginia Commonwealth University. He writes and performs with the United States Navy Band Commodores Jazz Ensemble in Washington, DC, and is highly sought after as a freelance performer. He has recorded three CDs under his own name. See www.robholmes.com.

Bil Jackson is the principal clarinetist with the Colorado Symphony Orchestra and the Aspen Chamber Symphony, and he previously performed as principal clarinetist with the Pittsburgh, St. Louis, Minnesota, Cincinnati, and Honolulu Orchestras, and has appeared as a soloist with the Colorado, Honolulu, Denver, Charlotte, Dallas Chamber, and Aspen Chamber orchestras. He is Professor of Clarinet at the University of Northern Colorado and is on the artist-faculty of the Aspen Music Festival. He is a Yamaha artist and is developing a new Yamaha clarinet.

Celeste Johnson is currently the Assistant Professor of Oboe at Oklahoma State University, and is also a member of the Tulsa Symphony Orchestra. She has performed extensively in competitions, including as a finalist in the Gillet-Fox International Oboe Competition, and in music festivals around the world, including Tanglewood, Aspen, Lucerne (Switzerland), Banff, Sarasota, and Kent/Blossom. She holds degrees from the Eastman School of Music and the University of Illinois at Urbana-Champaign.

Lynn Klock is Professor of Saxophone at the University of Massachusetts Amherst, and is bass clarinetist and saxophonist with the Springfield Symphony Orchestra. He is in demand as a Selmer clinician, and his recordings can be heard on the CRI, Gasparo, Albany, Open Loop, Orion, and Mark labels. He has premiered dozens of works written for and dedicated to him. He is a graduate of the Interlochen Arts Academy and the University of Michigan, where he studied with Lawrence Teal, Donald Sinta, and Jack Kripl.

Charles E. Lawson is Associate Professor and Coordinator of Woodwinds at Colorado State University. He earned his B.M.E. at the University of Kansas, and his M.A. degree and D.M.A. in clarinet performance and pedagogy at the University of Iowa. Dr. Lawson taught at Viterbo College, Drake University, Midwestern Music and Art Camp, and Blue Lake Fine Arts Camp. He has performed as clinician and soloist with many ensembles throughout the United States.

Kenneth Lee, clarinetist, has maintained a thriving independent studio in Vienna, Virginia for thirty-five years. A former member of the US Army Band, he has had five national first-place winners in MTNA competitions and was national chair of the Independent Music Teachers Forum of MTNA. Former students perform in the Washington Service Bands and teach independently and at the conservatory level.

Lewis Lipnick is principal contrabassoonist of the National Symphony Orchestra, and world premiered Gunther Schuller's *Contrabassoon Concerto* with the NSO in 1979. In February 2006, he commissioned, premiered, and recorded Kalevi Aho's *Contrabassoon Concerto* for the BIS recording label in Norway with the Bergen Philharmonic, then immediately went on to perform the Aho throughout Finland.

Joseph Lulloff is Distinguished Professor of Music at Michigan State University in East Lansing, Michigan. He has performed as a member of the wind sections of the Cleveland Orchestra, St. Louis Symphony Orchestra, Minnesota Orchestra, and Grand Rapids Symphony Orchestra, among others. He received the Teacher/Scholar Award from MSU and the Michigan State University Distinguished Faculty Award in 2006.

Bruce Marking is a clarinetist and a woodwind technician at Buffet-Crampon USA. As a clarinetist he performs with symphony orchestras in Florida and the southeastern United States. He holds a bachelor's degree in music education from New Mexico State University, a master's in clarinet performance from the University of Iowa, and has done doctoral work at Florida State University. His principal teachers include Himie Voxman, Charles West, and Frank Kowalsky.

Leslie Marrs is Assistant Professor of Flute at Drake University in Des Moines, Iowa, and earned degrees from the University of North Carolina at Greensboro (DMA), Florida State University (MM), and Virginia Commonwealth University (BM). She is also a member of the College Music Society Contemporary Chamber Players and former soloist with the United States Army Field Band.

James Mason is highly regarded as one of Canada's most prominent oboists and teachers. Since 1979 he has been the principal oboe of the Kitchener-Waterloo Symphony and Canadian Chamber Ensemble. He has appeared as a soloist, chamber musician, and clinician around the world. He is on the faculty at Wilfrid Laurier University.

Steve McNeal taught band and choir in the Eaton schools upon graduation from the University of Northern Colorado, and subsequently taught orchestra in the Ft. Collins schools from 1962 until his retirement in 1998. He has conducted several all-state orchestras, and is the recipient of National Teacher of the Year awards from MENC (1987–1988) and ASTA (1997–1998). The McNeal Performing Arts Center at the new Ft. Collins High School was named in his honor.

Gary Moody teaches double reeds and theory at Colorado State University. He holds B.A. and B.M. degrees from the University of Northern Colorado, an M.F.A. from the University of Iowa, and a D.A. from the University of Northern Colorado. He has been a member of the Des Moines Symphony, the National Repertory Orchestra, and the Orchestra of the Nico Milan Opera House in Cape Town, South Africa. He is principal bassoon with the Breckenridge Music Festival Orchestra in Breckenridge, Colorado.

Ricardo Morales became principal clarinet of the Metropolitan Opera Orchestra in 1993 at age twenty-one, and in 2002, was appointed principal clarinet of the Philadelphia Orchestra. A native of Puerto Rico, he is heard widely as a soloist and has performed at the Kennedy

Center, the Metropolitan Museum of Art Concert Series, the Chamber Music Society of Lincoln Center, and on NBC's *Today*. Morales currently serves on the faculties of the Juilliard School, Manhattan School of Music, and the Verbier Academy in Switzerland.

Christine A. Moran, M.S., P.T., C.H.T. is the director of James River Hand Therapy located in Midlothian, Virginia (Richmond). She is a specialist trained in physical therapy and hand therapy with over twenty-five years of experience treating musicians. She has been a lecturer and an author of hand therapy topics. She also had academic appointments at Medical College of Virginia, Old Dominion University, and Rocky Mountain University.

Paige Morgan is currently Associate Professor of Oboe at Ithaca College. She also serves on the faculty of the Brevard Music Center Festival, where she has played principal English horn and 2nd oboe for the past eleven years. She received her doctor of musical arts and master of music degrees and performer's certificate from the Eastman School of Music.

Lynn Ann Musco has held the position of Professor of Clarinet and Woodwind Coordinator at Stetson University since 1988. She is an artist/clinician for Leblanc Division of the Conn-Selmer Corporation, maintains a studio of approximately forty university and private students, and is an active soloist, chamber musician, and orchestral performer.

James Nesbit is an active performer on all members of the saxophone, clarinet, flute, and bassoon families, and has appeared as a soloist with the Virginia Symphony and at Carnegie Hall. His very diverse performing credits include such artists as Tony Bennett, Al Jarreau, and Lynyrd Skynyrd, in addition to opera, ballet, and symphony orchestras. Mr. Nesbit is on the faculties of Old Dominion University, the College of William and Mary, Hampton University, and Chowan University.

Sheri Oyan is a saxophonist and founder of both the *quux* saxophone quartet and the multimedia new music ensemble *quux* collective. She holds a D.M.A. in Saxophone Performance from Louisiana State University and has served as an adjunct saxophone professor at Northwestern State University (2002–2007) and Virginia Commonwealth University (1999–2002 and 2008–).

Elsie Parker is a woodwind doubler on clarinets, flutes, and saxophones in the St. Louis MUNY Opera and FOX Theater Orchestras, and is an extra clarinetist with the St. Louis Symphony Orchestra. As a professional vocalist, she has recorded three CDs of popular French songs, has sung in the St. Louis area, in Chicago, San Francisco, and on French television, and she performs regularly with her own group, The Poor People of Paris. Elsie he has been vocal soloist with numerous symphony orchestras in Missouri, Florida, and Illinois.

Richard Polonchak was formerly the principal bassoonist of the US Marine Band, "The President's Own," and the White House Orchestra in Washington, DC. He has taught at eight universities and currently teaches at Shepherd University in Shepherdstown, West Virginia. His articles on all aspects of the bassoon have appeared in *The Instrumentalist*, *The School Musician*, *Woodwind World*, *The Double Reed*, and *Bandworld* magazines. He is the author of *Primary Handbook for Bassoon*.

Richard Ramey, versed in classical, jazz, and Latin-American music, is Professor of Bassoon at the University of Arkansas. He is a member of the Tulsa Symphony, the orchestras of the Tulsa Ballet, Opera, and Oratorio, the Lyrique Quintette, and Olor a Café. He has performed throughout the US, Europe, and Asia, and has authored several articles and two books on bassoon performance. He also performs on the theremin. His degrees are from Arizona State University and the University of Southern California.

Albert Regni, principal saxophonist of the New York Philharmonic, the New York City Ballet, and formerly of the Metropolitan Opera, has appeared with the Leningrad, Odessa, St. Petersburg, Israel, Baltimore, Los Angeles, National Symphony, Rotterdam, and American Composer's Orchestras. As a New York City studio musician for many years, he received a Gold Record for his solos on the television series *Twin Peaks*, performed on more than fifty major movies, twenty Broadway cast albums, and a vast number of recordings of classical, chamber, jazz, and television commercials.

Ibby Roberts is the principal bassoonist and outreach coordinator of the Charlottesville Symphony Orchestra. She serves on the music performance faculty at the University of Virginia, and she enjoys an active freelance life with several orchestras, including the National Symphony Orchestra, the Richmond Symphony, and the Virginia Symphony. She enjoys teaching private lessons in bassoon, oboe, reed making, and chamber music.

Eugene Rousseau, Artist Professor at the University of Minnesota, is Distinguished Professor Emeritus at the Indiana University Jacobs School of Music. He has appeared as a soloist and teacher throughout the world, and has numerous recordings and publications to his credit. A Fulbright scholar, he studied saxophone at the Paris Conservatory with Marcel Mule. He earned the Ph.D. degree at the University of Iowa, where his teacher was Himie Voxman.

Rebecca Kemper Scarnati is Professor of Oboe at Northern Arizona University. Dr. Scarnati is principal oboist of the Flagstaff Symphony, oboist for the Kokopelli Ensemble, and performs with the Desert Foothills Music Fest in Carefree, Arizona. She has performed with many orchestras across the United States and toured for three years in the United States and Europe as the oboist with the Con Spirito Woodwind Quintet.

Helen Ann Shanley is Professor of Flute and Chamber Music at Baylor University. As a soloist and founding member of the Baylor Woodwind Quintet, she has given master classes and recitals throughout the US and in China, Costa Rica, Belgium, Mexico, Panama, and Venezuela. Her students are performing and teaching throughout the United States and in China. In 1992 she was chosen Outstanding Creative Artist at Baylor University.

Richard Shanley is Professor of Clarinet and coordinator of the Woodwind Department at Baylor University, where he is a founding member of the Baylor Quintet and was voted an outstanding tenured professor. He has extensive professional experience and has presented recitals and classes in North, Central, and South America, China, Canada, England, and Europe. His primary teachers are Ronald Phillips, Dr. Lee Gibson, Robert Marcellus, and Larry Combs.

Kenneth Singleton is Director of Bands at the University of Northern Colorado in Greeley. He has more than thirty published wind ensemble and band transcriptions to his credit, and his critical editions of Charles Ives' music have been recorded by the Chicago Symphony, St. Louis Symphony, San Francisco Symphony, and numerous other orchestras. He has been working with student double woodwind quintets (and their permutations) since 1976.

Guido Six studied at the Royal Conservatory of Music in Gent, where he obtained many first prizes, as well as a higher diploma and master's degree in clarinet performance. He was the principal clarinet of the Band of the Belgian Police for ten years and then changed to education. Since 1994 he is the director of the Conservatory in Ostend. He is the only person to have organized two ClarinetFests for ICA and he is also the founder/conductor of the worldwide known clarinet choir Claribel.

Robert Spring has been described as "one of this country's most sensitive and talented clarinetists." Spring attended the University of Michigan, where he earned three degrees, including the D.M.A. He was recently awarded the "Citation of Merit Award" from the School of Music Alumni Society. He was President of the International Clarinet Association from 1998–2000. He is Professor of Clarinet at Arizona State University and is principal clarinet of the ProMusic Chamber Orchestra of Columbus, Ohio.

Steven Stusek teaches saxophone at the University of North Carolina–Greensboro. He has degrees from Indiana University, Arizona State University, and the Conservatoire de la Cite de Paris. His teachers include Eugene Rousseau, Daniel Deffayet, Joe Wytko, Larry Teal, and David Baker. He is currently President of the North American Saxophone Alliance.

Dale Underwood, one of the foremost classical saxophonists of all time, was longtime soloist with the US Navy Band. He has been soloist with the Boston Pops, National Symphony, and numerous other orchestras, and in 1993 he made his Carnegie Hall debut. Many of his numerous recordings are pieces written for him. He is Professor of Saxophone at George Mason University the Universities of Maryland and Miami, and is past-president of the North America Saxophone Alliance.

Himie Voxman is the author and compiler of many widely used methods and studies for wind instruments and has edited numerous solos and ensembles. He holds a bachelor's degree in chemical engineering and a master's in psychology of music. His studies were with Carl Seashore, William Gower, Sr., Gustave Langenus, and Clarence Warmelin. Mr. Voxman was director of the School of Music at the University of Iowa from 1954 to 1980.

Michael Webster is Professor of Clarinet at Rice University's Shepherd School of Music and Artistic Director of the Houston Youth Symphony. Formerly principal clarinetist with the Rochester Philharmonic and the San Francisco Symphony, he has appeared with the Chamber Music Society of Lincoln Center, Da Camera of Houston, the 92nd Street "Y," the Tokyo, Cleveland, Ying, and Muir String Quartets, and many of North America's leading festivals.

John Weigand teaches clarinet and conducts the Chamber Winds at West Virginia University. He performs with the Baltimore Symphony and the Laureate Quintet, and is principal clarinetist of the Seneca Chamber Orchestra. Dr. Weigand holds degrees from Florida State and Northwestern Universities and the Oberlin Conservatory, where his principal teachers have included Robert Marcellus, Fred Ormand, Lawrence McDonald, Keith Stein, and Kent Krive.

Mark Weiger is Professor of Oboe at the University of Iowa, a member of the double reed consort WiZARDS!, and an international soloist and recording artist. Weiger is also an associate director for the University of Iowa School of Music and named a University Collegiate Fellow. With over a dozen CDs to his credit, he has published book chapters through Schirmer and Simon & Schuster, and has published more than thirty chamber works.

Charles West has been called "the most widely recorded clarinetist in American academia." He is heard on labels including Klavier, Wilson Audiophile, Centaur and CRI, and on a Grammy award–winning Telarc release. He performs on flute, oboe, saxophone, and clarinet, and is Professor of Clarinet at Virginia Commonwealth University. West has been a Fulbright scholar, is past-president of the International Clarinet Association, and is editor of the current volume.

Preparing a Professional Oboist

Ann Adams

INGREDIENTS:
Two measures discipline
One measure setting goals
One measure creating strategies
One measure developing good habits
One measure passion for music
Shake vigorously until frothy; top off with commitment and dedication.

SERVES:
Anyone who strives to become a successful professional musician and teacher.

Becoming a successful musician and teacher requires more than the fundamentals of playing the oboe. It is imperative to be passionate for what you do. I believe that I am a teacher every minute of my life, whether I am performing a recital, attending a concert, or giving a lesson. It is important to be a positive role model in every aspect.

In addition to teaching my students the fundamentals of playing the oboe and developing their musical skills, I consider it my responsibility to expand the student's vision, to expose the student to a genuine enthusiasm for music, and to set a foundation for success in life. As a teacher, I emphasize philosophy and constantly encourage my students to develop a personal philosophy that will permeate every aspect of their lives.

Establish Discipline

Nothing meaningful comes without discipline and hard work. If you look closely at all great musicians and teachers, one common trait that they all have is a strong work ethic. These musicians have an intense motivation to succeed and they always remain focused on that aspiration. We all have the desire to be the best in our fields, but we do not always take the steps required to achieve that desire. It is easy to say that we want to be the best, but the true test is determined by how committed we are to reach that level. Learn how to fight through the adversity we all encounter in life and challenge yourself to accomplish things you never dreamed possible. Being highly motivated, disciplined, and dedicated to your profession are fundamental qualities for your success.

First of all, look closely at your actions. How hard do you work? Are you organized? Do you maintain discipline in your life? It is essential to establish a solid work ethic and strategies in order to excel as a musician. Write down your goals and discuss them with people whom you respect. Create a plan and follow the advice of your teacher, perhaps the one person closest to you who has experience in moving students from one level to the next. Developing this kind of discipline and focus will result in realizing your goals. Your teacher is perhaps your best ally to help you achieve your goals and overcome your challenges.

If you truly aspire to work at your highest level you will create a sense of self esteem that will help you believe in yourself and facilitate your desire to push yourself beyond what you ever thought possible. When you reach a setback, the first thing to do is figure out what it will take to overcome your obstacle. Establish strategies and develop a timeline for how and when you will conquer that challenge. Take the responsibility to figure out for yourself what you need to do—practice carefully, pay attention to detail, and develop a systematic way to practice with consistency. Schedule your practice time when you can concentrate without distractions. You owe it to yourself to take pride in what you do and to do everything possible to work at the highest level. Nothing does more for your self esteem than the confidence you gain when you can do what is expected of you.

Set Goals
Setting goals will help develop your strategies and will provide achievable objectives for improvement. In order to be your best, you must not practice aimlessly. It is a critical fundamental for improvement to make a plan for how you will progress. Take an honest look at your strengths and weaknesses and work with what you already have to take your playing to the next level. It is natural to want to work on what comes easily and avoid that which is difficult. Address issues that are more difficult first. It is important to set demanding goals that are going to help you overcome your weaknesses. Don't set unrealistic goals, but don't set your standards too low either. The key is to continually reevaluate your goals, which will allow you to reach your full potential.

Keep a practice journal and write down step by step what it will take to accomplish your vision. You need to be organized and establish short-term as well as long-term objectives. Organize your day by establishing a systematic plan and setting specific goals. You should decide what you want to accomplish and determine what methods you are going to use. Start each practice session with a purpose; end each session evaluating your accomplishments and developing a practice schedule for the next day. By making a daily plan you are instantly establishing a foundation and structure to your practice routine.

Reaching your goals will enable you to have faith in your abilities and develop self-confidence. Don't allow obstacles or difficulties to dominate your life. Be positive and self-motivated. If you are passionate for what you are doing, your "work" will become what you love to do. If you are highly motivated to do well, you will be excited about everything you do and always work to be the best you can be. When you approach life with a positive attitude you tend to attract others with the same desires, which is very exciting and stimulating. You should always generate an aura of excitement and enthusiasm for what you are doing. Immerse yourself into what you are trying to become. Listen to music, read about music, attend concerts, recitals, and master classes, and associate with other musicians by participating in your professional organizations.

Develop Good Habits
Coming to your lesson or rehearsals unprepared is obvious and frustrating for the teacher/conductor, so schedule practice time every day. Your time gets more unmanageable as the day progresses. Develop your habit to practice in the morning when you are more alert and you have fewer distractions. So many students tend to put off their practice time to the evening,

when they are tired and unable to focus. Be sure to get enough rest and maintain a healthy diet and lifestyle. It takes a lot of energy to stay focused and to work at your peak. These habits will guard against underachieving and help you reach your goals.

Pay attention to people who are already successful. You can learn through their experiences. People all around you (professors, friends, other students) have things to teach you—you need to be receptive to them. It is easy to be closed minded with respect to whom you choose for your role models—not even taking into consideration what you can learn from your contemporaries. Look to role models as people you can emulate, people from whom you can learn, and people for whom you have a great amount of respect. It is important to select the right role models. Be sure to seek out people who can help you and who will support and encourage you to be the best you can be.

As you set your goals and develop your own philosophy by which you live, not only will you improve as a performer and person—you will become one that will motivate and inspire others. ➤●

(Acknowledgment: Ideas for developing a personal philosophy come from the book: *Success is a Choice* by Rick Pitino.)

Tasteful Oboe Playing—Developing the Fundamentals of Tone

Valarie Anderson

INGREDIENTS:
Intelligence, good ears, and curiosity

SERVES:
All oboists and people who listen to them.

The oboe is often referred to as "the ill wind that no one plays well." It is sometimes likened to the sound of a duck and, unfortunately, that is what many young oboists sound like, through no fault of their own. Most public school band directors have had very little preparation for teaching oboe—often as little as a few weeks of instruction in their undergraduate woodwind techniques classes. No one can expect the average music teacher to deal with the intricacies of adjusting oboe reeds, one of the major obstacles for the oboist. However, teachers should know about the characteristics of a good reed and embouchure formation in order to guide their young students.

Reed Selection (The Most Important Ingredient of Our Recipe)
A poorly constructed reed will handicap a young student. A good reed will eliminate barriers and allow one to perform all the requirements of the music. It must have pitch stability, dynamic flexibility, and response. The following is not meant as a reed adjustment guide, but simply as a list of characteristics of a good reed. Until students can make their own reeds, they will need to purchase finished reeds. Ideally, only reeds with all of these qualities should be used, or the student may develop poor habits by making incorrect physical adjustments in the embouchure.

Important physical attributes of good reeds include:

Oboe reed tip

A good reed will have the same appearance when it is dry as when it is wet. Even when dry, the sides should be together. While looking at the tip opening, you want to see an even arch. Players should not need to frequently squeeze the reed sides to try to keep it open. The proper reed tip shape is shown to the left.

The lay of the reed is all of the territory that is scraped.

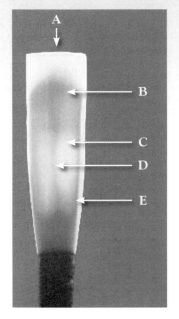

The tip (letter A) begins where the main strength of the reed ends. The tip sets the reed in vibration and the length of the tip determines the length of the entire reed. If the tip is too long in comparison to the rest of the reed, the reed will be unstable; if it is too short, the reed is inflexible.

The plateau (letter B) holds the reed opening, keeps the high notes up in pitch, and gives stability to the reed.

The "ribs" or "windows" (letter C) produce lower partials and deepen tone quality.

The "spine" (letter D) and "rails" or "sides" (letter E) give the reed structure and strength. They must support the reed but must have flexibility. If either is scraped too much, the reed will lose the basic vibration. If too much cane is removed from the spine, the reed will sound hollow.

The shape of the reed should not flare at the tip. Any widening at this point sacrifices the high register. If the reed flares, it is impossible to achieve the correct pitches of the crow.

A very important aspect of the reed is that the sides seal tightly all the way to the tip. Any leaking along the sides will reduce the stability and response of the reed. When the sides are properly sealed, there is no need for fish skin or wire. The use of either inhibits the vibration of the reed. To test the seal of the reed, place a finger over the end of the tube and blow the reed with the embouchure near the tip. There should be no air escaping through the sides.

The "crow" of the reed is an indication of how the reed is vibrating and is an important technique that each oboist needs to learn. By placing the reed in your mouth with the lips

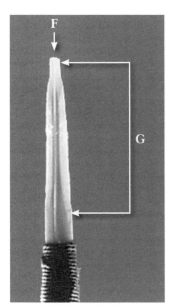

touching the thread, slowly start blowing the air without any articulation. The first sound should be a high C and as you add more air pressure the lower octave Cs will become present in the crow. If the crow is below pitch, the reed will play flat. If the lower Cs of the crow are not present, the reed will have a tendency to go sharp. A properly constructed reed that has pitch stability should crow the same at the end of a practice session as at the beginning, provided the embouchure is correct.

The profile of the reed should show a gradual slope into the tip (letter F). There must be elements of both connection and separation. If there is too much blend, the reed loses flexibility and pitch. If there is too much separation, the reed produces mostly tip vibrations (reedy, buzzy sound).

When looking at the profile, you should see a straight line from the bark through the plateau area (area G). If a dip is seen, too much cane has been removed and the reed loses vibrations.

5

Third-line B is the true indicator of the pitch of the reed. This can be tested by playing a low B with a fairly loose embouchure and slurring to the B one octave higher while maintaining the same embouchure. (N.B. Be certain that you are not changing embouchure and have proper diaphragm support.) In this test you are comparing the entire length of the tube to the shortest length. If the octave is not in tune and the upper B is flat, the reed lacks pitch stability and the player will end up using the embouchure to manipulate the reed in an attempt to correct the pitch.

To test the response of the reed, blow the lowest G with a fairly loose embouchure and no tongue. The tone should start easily with very little lip pressure. A minimum of air noise should precede the tone, like when saying or singing "who."

When the oboe reed has proper pitch stability, one should be able to play any note throughout the range of the instrument without manipulating the embouchure, provided the instrument itself is correctly tuned.

Let us now talk about the proper oboe embouchure and diaphragm support (the next ingredients of our recipe).

The oboe embouchure is similar to whistling, with the corners of the lips pushing forwards to anchor the embouchure. The mouth should be open with approximately one-half inch between the teeth. Have the student form their embouchure first by saying "OH" pushing forward on the corners of the mouth. While maintaining that position, say "EE" which points the position of the chin downward. Place the reed on the lower lip and let the upper lip come down into place. The upper lip should be slightly in front of the lower lip, giving more control over tone. If the lips are directly opposite each other, the sound will be deadened. The lips should not be rolled in, as this will cause too much flesh to touch the reed, thus muffling the sound. Frequently young students will do this to compensate for a poor reed. If the reed is too noisy and bright, a discriminating student will try to control the sound by putting more flesh on the reed or playing on the very tip. They can sometimes produce a more covered tone, but they will have limited dynamic range and articulation.

The flesh holding the reed must not be soft or loose. The muscles along the corners of the mouth must be flexed. The oboist should be able to hold the reed alone in their mouth (without the help of the fingers) and do repeated staccato quarter notes with no movement of the reed. This tests the amount of flex and control of the corner muscles. Players at all ages should do this in front of a mirror. The pitch produced is approximately C. Too little reed in the mouth will result in a lower pitch and too much teeth pressure will produce a higher pitch.

In all of this, proper diaphragm support is assumed. However, too many young students compensate for improper support by pinching the reed. Once again, have the student play with the reed alone in the mouth (no oboe) and play staccato quarters. But also have them press against their stomach, striving for a constant diaphragm pressure.

The strength of the embouchure must be built up and developed over time. The student should not play beyond the point that they can play with comfort.

Selecting the Proper Oboe (The Frosting for Our Recipe)
A good, properly maintained instrument is the final ingredient for our recipe. The oboe should have the full conservatory plateau system, with the left hand F key, the forked F resonance key, and the low B-flat key, allowing the student to develop the proper technique

from the beginning. A frequent problem with lower-level oboes is that the student must learn alternate fingerings to correct for pitch and tone. The most common of these is the addition of the E-flat key for "forked" F. Later when they do get a better instrument with an automatic resonant F, they must break their established habit of adding the extra key.

The better quality oboes will have "fraised" or "under-cut" tone holes, which contribute to a more even scale on the instrument. All of the pads, with the possible exception of low B and B-flat, should be made from cork, in order to obtain the best seal possible. Additionally, when different types of pads are mixed, it can lead to unevenness in the tone and scale.

Unfortunately, oboes do go out of adjustment fairly easily. There are close to twenty small adjustment screws on the oboe, which control the balance of the keys. These adjustments need to be checked regularly to ensure that all the pads are sealing correctly. The slightest leak will lead to problems in response.

In conclusion, with the combination of a stable reed, proper embouchure, and a good instrument, this recipe, when followed for several years, will produce a delicious oboe tone, suitable for solo or ensemble playing.

Bon appétit! ➜

Bananas, Turkey, and Almonds—A Studio Teacher's Recipe for Coaching a Successful Recital

Shelley Binder

Preparing a student for a full recital is an arduous endeavor. A studio teacher's duties range from choosing appropriate repertoire and encouraging healthy practice habits to providing a nurturing environment and helping manage a multitude of important details.

INGREDIENTS:

One of the most helpful tools is a practice book. The practice book consists of a three-ring binder containing separate sections for a schedule and photocopies of each piece of music that needs to be learned. Photocopying the music allows the student to keep the original in good condition and to make subsequent clean copies after the initial marking is no longer needed.

The next step is to divide each piece into manageable sections. Number each section and determine the baseline tempo based on the lowest speed at which all finger technique is clean and relaxed. Next have the student study the music carefully and mark any details that might be missed during a performance. These details include breath marks, accidentals, articulations, and reminders to take a sip of water. I call this step "marking" the music. Also important are what I refer to as "left hand notes." These are important reminders that you write in the upper left-hand corner of the music and need to get into the habit of always looking at before playing. These might include: "pull out" or "push in," "relax hands" or "remember to open music."

Determining each student's learning style is the important next step in planning a practice strategy. For instance, if a student is an auditory learner, it is helpful for them to record each lesson and practice session and to listen to as many professional recordings as they can find. Don't forget that the Internet is a great source for finding various recordings to download. If the student is mainly a visual learner, marking the music in creative ways may help. For instance, breath marks in red, articulations in blue, etc. If you have a student who is a kinesthetic learner, it is important to have them lay out their practice sessions carefully so they do not over-practice and get repetitive stress injuries. A good strategy here is to encourage them to practice for 45 minutes per hour with 15-minute breaks for stretching and relaxation, and to spread these practice sessions throughout the day.

A practice club is a helpful tool. Each week I set up a minimum of two practice club sessions. I give extra credit for each session but attendance is voluntary. These sessions are always well attended and well received. Each person chooses one lick, generally 2–4 measures in length, that they would like to work on. Each person plays the excerpt, after which the group discusses the inherent difficulties and offers opinions on how to conquer the challenges. I am always there to lead the discussions and reiterate my advice of breaking down the lick into smaller fragments and applying practice rhythms (e.g., long-short-long-short-long, then reversing the pattern to short-long-short-long and finally long-short-short-long long-short-short-long), playing the lick forward and backward then playing as written slowly and successively speeding up the tempo. I always stress that there is a quotient for each individual person with each individual lick. The quotient is the number of practice sessions or days at which each individual must practice each individual lick before the lick is totally secure. If, at a later time, the student continues to miss the lick, I reassure them that they have not "reached their quotient" and must continue practicing using practice rhythms.

It is at this point that an excellent opportunity to "practice for performance" is often missed. This step is crucial for ensuring that small mistakes in performance do not snowball into larger catastrophes. There are always small mistakes that are made in performances due to nerves, and this is to be expected. There is a technique for learning how to handle those mistakes and continue without any indication that there was an error. It is human nature to be disappointed when you make a mistake on stage but it is imperative to learn how to appropriately manage your response so that you are not thrown off when this occurs.

I practice this by employing the use of a practice abacus. A practice abacus is a string with four beads. (A simpler version could be made using four pennies on the stand or four Tums—whichever seems appropriate.) After practicing with the practice rhythms for perfection, it is important to practice for performance using the abacus. Play the lick, visualizing that you are on stage and the only thing that is important is to play the lick with no hesitations, seamlessly incorporating any mistakes into the phrase. Correcting mistakes is not important at this point. So if you play the lick without grimacing at the mistakes, stopping to berate yourself, or showing dissatisfaction, you get to move one bead to the right. Repeat this step making sure to act as though you are in front of an audience. If, however, your temper gets the better of you and you stop at a mistake, pull the tempo, or indicate your displeasure, you must move all the beads back over to the left and start the process over.

A helpful way to work with your students on acquiring a more positive attitude is to have two cans in your studio. One labeled "expletives, negative remarks, insults, self-deprecating comments, bad vibes, self-destructive-self-mutilating-self-esteem-depleting words" and the other labeled "positive affirmations and self-esteem." I incorporate a point system for counting the negative comments against their grade and rewarding them for positive comments. It is sometimes shocking to a new student how many negative comments they make about themselves in lessons. I write each comment on a sticky note, being careful to attribute the comment to the student and place it in the can. Often, a student will begin to say something negative and, realizing the consequences, will modify their pronouncement in a positive way.

It is important that you talk about visualization early on in this process. I employ a tactic that I refer to as "the water cure." I encourage all my students to carry a container of water with them. Each time you take a sip of water, you are to visualize some aspect of the upcoming performance and say "I can do this," then visualizing another aspect, say "I CAN do this." You continue visualizing different elements of the recital, each day shifting the mantra to "I can DO this" and "I can do THIS."

At this point I start discussing the development of "the plan." This is a technique for examining every expectation that you and your student have for the recital. Sit down and talk about how the student feels about his or her progress and try to get them to imagine that the recital has just finished and they are backstage packing up their instrument. Ask them what would make them feel good at that moment. A perfect, flawless recital where every detail was exactly as they imagined it?

It might happen, but chances are that there will likely be a few mistakes and a few unforeseen emergencies that will have to be dealt with. You have to convince them that the mistakes are factored into "the plan" and that they need to prepare themselves mentally for anything that might be thrown at them at the last moment (a flat tire on the way to the hall, a rip in their dress, etc.) You have to encourage them to believe that they will be happy with the recital in spite of all possible outcomes if they just follow "the plan." "Nobody ever plans to fail; they just fail to plan."

An important step is to have your students perform regularly at low-pressure venues, including nursing homes, religious services, and anywhere else they are likely to receive positive feedback. These performances are crucial for compiling what I refer to as "the lexicon of performing maladies." Adrenaline affects individuals differently and it is important to note each individual physiological response and strategy for managing it. For example, my lexicon contains my performing maladies and strategies for overcoming them:

1. **Dry mouth.** Glycerin spray and biotin gum, both available over-the-counter from any pharmacy, to treat dry mouth.
2. **Cold hands.** Heating pad backstage.
3. **Nerves.** Carbohydrate meal (pasta) several hours before recital; banana 45 minutes to an hour before recital.

Planning that needs to take place at least *a week* before recital:
    Reception
    Page-turner
    Recording engineer
    Stage manager
    Programs

Things that must be done at least *three days* prior include:
    Writing thank-you notes to accompanist, page turner, reception hosts
    Buy foods to help with nerves (bananas, turkey, almonds, etc.)

Things to consider about the *dress rehearsal*:
    If you plan on having water or glycerin spray on stage during the recital, you must have them at the dress rehearsal and practice using them during rests and between movements.
    If you are wearing new shoes, be sure to scuff the soles with sandpaper or on pavement and wear them during the dress rehearsal.
    Practice preparing and eating a high-carbohydrate meal a few hours before, and then bananas, turkey, or almonds 45 minutes to an hour before dress rehearsal.

Things to consider *the day before* the recital:
    Exercise and relax as you normally do.
    Drink ample amounts of water while visualizing different elements of the recital and saying, "I can do this, I CAN do this, I can DO this, and I can do THIS."
    Only practice difficult licks slowly—this is not the time to sabotage yourself by playing everything at a breakneck tempo and risking mistakes.

Compile all articles that will be necessary for the recital and that will be going to the hall with you, including: music, clothes, thank-you notes, check for accompanist's fee, food for nerves, extra blank CDs for the recording engineer, programs, heating pad, cup for water.

Things to do *the day of* the recital:
Keep talking to a minimum, as this tends to dry out your mouth.
Give your cell phone to a friend to manage last-minute questions and directions by well-meaning but distracting family members.
Get to the hall at least 45 minutes in advance.
Long hair must be pulled up out of your face.

Avoid *self-sabotage*:
Do not do anything new or out of the ordinary, such as wearing lipstick when you normally don't. Do not spend most of the day in a salon getting a manicure and hair extensions. Do not wear four-inch heels that you just bought and have no experience performing in. Do not wear anything tight, binding, uncomfortable, or dramatically low cut. Do not eat a heavy meal out at a restaurant with all of your out-of-town relatives.

***After the recital*:**
Remember to be gracious. The only appropriate response to a compliment is THANK YOU!

SERVES:
Studio teachers and students preparing to present a full recital.

Developing Facility on the Bass Clarinet

J. Lawrie Bloom

INGREDIENTS:
You need a bass clarinet that is in playable condition (too often a "school" instrument is not in playing condition and a young player gets blamed when no one could be expected to play it), a player with the intellectual curiosity to want to add the bass clarinet to his/her musical bag of tricks, and a little assistance to get started.

SERVES:
Bass clarinetists, and their conductors and colleagues.

Preparation:
Putting together a bass clarinet is different than putting together a B-flat clarinet. There are more long rods that can get bent, and more bridge keys that need to be positioned correctly before putting the joints together so that they are not knocked out of adjustment or have the corks torn off. Start by putting the bell on the bottom joint, taking care to set the bridge key on a low C bass so that it does not get bent. On a Buffet instrument that means closing the key on the bell (thereby raising the bridge key). On other makers' instruments this may be slightly different, so look at the way the bridge goes together before you try to assemble each joint. (Sufficient cork grease should always be applied, so that you don't have to force the pieces together.) I hold the bell with my right hand, and hold the bottom joint with my left. This allows me to reach around the keys of the lower joint, applying no pressure to the long keys and rods, which can most easily bend.

Next add the top joint. Holding the joint with the left hand, depress the throat A key, and the D/A key. This raises the back bridge key and lowers the front bridge key, making it possible to slide the two joints together without hurting any of the four parts of the bridges.

Now, add the mouthpiece to the neck, which gives you a nice "handle" while you put on the reed and ligature. Finally, put the neck on the top joint, starting with the upper-register key out to the side, then swing it gently in. If the bass is set up correctly, the top register key should have space between it and the arm that sticks up to activate it. Not much, but it needs a little or you'll never know when you might end up in the upper register by accident. Now put the endpin in and adjust to your height. The correct height should allow you to bring the instrument in to your embouchure without you adjusting your head, neck, or spine.

Stirring:
Now let's get to making sounds on the instrument.

I am fortunate to present numerous master classes each year, mostly on college campuses, on clarinet and bass clarinet. Inevitably the question is asked, "What do you have to do differently on bass clarinet than on clarinet?"

I think this is actually the wrong question for most players. Especially for college level or advanced high school players, the question should be, "What do we do the same as playing a clarinet to play bass clarinet?"

In this way you are approaching a new member of the clarinet family from strength and experience, rather than from fear and confusion.

When beginning any member of the clarinet family with which you are unaccustomed, I suggest you start with scales. Whether bass, E-flat, basset horn, or whatever, most players squeak in the beginning not because they are doing something wrong with their embouchures, but because they hit the wrong key at the wrong time. Just grazing a key not needed for the note you are playing can give you some fabulous loud, high squeaks and squawks. I use the Klosé scales that many of us learned as children. In the beginning you don't need extended range scales, so they work just fine.

In my experience, when most clarinet players are presented with a bass clarinet, they look at this large instrument and immediately overblow. While the bass clarinet bore is bigger than the clarinet bore, the aperture—the opening between the reed and the mouthpiece—is only slightly larger. Blowing too much air only causes the reed to vibrate out of control and the sound becomes unfocused—somewhat like a foghorn.

On virtually every horn I have played, the low F is a pretty good note. Begin with a slow, relaxed flow of air and play a low F, listening for a good sound. It should be rich, round, and free. It should take very little effort to produce this note. When you have a good sound from the low F, begin to slowly play an upward scale. Make sure you to go very slowly so that you can compare each note, keeping that rich, resonant sound as you change notes. Any advanced soprano clarinet player knows that there are minute resistance changes from note to note on the clarinet. The same is true on the bass, but these resistance changes may occur in different places than they do on the B-flat clarinet. All fine players make minute changes in the embouchure and airflow to adjust these notes on the soprano clarinet and make them match in timbre, dynamic, and color. This is also true on bass clarinet, so we just need to find where the resistance changes are on the instrument you are playing. Now, you may be waiting for me to tell you where they are. Each major company's instruments are different, and even individual instruments within the same company will vary slightly, so I can't do that. By slow playing, really listening as you go note to note, you will be able to identify them yourself. One reminder: don't overadjust. These changes have to be small enough that you can actually execute them when performing. If you find that you have to make huge changes in embouchure pressure or airflow to change the sound or pitch, then the instrument may need repair or replacement.

Baking:
After you are comfortable playing scales and beginning to find the resistance differences on the bass clarinet, almost any material will get you going. I like to start students off on Strauss tone poems, because they quickly help you to know what the instrument is capable of, and how it should sound. Each of the parts is so beautifully written for the bass clarinet that you will quickly gain great facility by working through them.

Many advanced clarinet players are not comfortable reading in bass clef, and Strauss' *Death and Transfiguration* presents us with a part mostly in bass clef. Try reading Bach *Cello Suites* to develop your bass clef reading. These are much less chromatic than the Strauss, so you will know if you are right or not. It really is necessary to read bass clef to perform on the bass clarinet, so hard work to hone this skill is time well spent.

Proceed without fear:
Another question I am all too frequently asked is "Will playing the bass clarinet ruin my clarinet playing?"

I have found in my own playing, when I first began to play bass, and in the playing of countless students with whom I have worked, that performing on bass clarinet only helps your clarinet playing. Why? It is impossible to play the bass with tension. The reed simply refuses to vibrate freely if there is tension present in the embouchure, the air stream, or the body. Learning to play without tension makes playing the bass possible, and this can only help your clarinet playing as well.

So go ahead and experiment. Try something you have always played on clarinet on the bass clarinet. I sometimes find I like certain clarinet pieces better on bass clarinet than clarinet, just because it allows a sound difference I find more satisfying for that particular piece.

Heard an interesting piece played by a bassoonist? Try it out. Feeling really brave? Check out some of the many, many pieces written for Josef Horak, Harry Spaarnay, or Michael Lowenstern. Nowadays there's a lot of music for the bass clarinet for solo, chamber, or large ensemble situations. You don't want to stop playing the incredible repertoire for the clarinet; you just want to add to it the amazing music and sounds of the bass clarinet. �־●

Breathing Demystified: A Recipe for Success

Leone Buyse

It seems so obvious. Breath is the essence of life, and fine wind playing depends on developing excellent breath control. Efficient, well-planned breathing allows wind players to connect with the music they're playing and to project their ideas with confidence. Citing the obvious parallel with singing is an apt approach, particularly for flutists; we don't contend with reeds but rather color the sound solely by controlling and shaping the air column with the embouchure and oral cavity. Yet how easy it is to take breathing for granted and focus instead on such other significant aspects of instrumental mastery as finger technique, articulation, embouchure, intonation, rhythm, and sight-reading. For wind players of all ages, learning and practicing the fundamentals of breathing can literally mean the difference between frustration and success.

INGREDIENTS:
Willing students with attentive minds and bodies
Observant mentors

SERVES:
All wind students, their teachers and ensemble directors (and ultimately, their audiences).

The gifted young flutist begins to play a difficult piece at his first lesson of the school year. His fingers move quickly and accurately, and it's clear that he enjoys the music he's playing. His first breath, however, is both noisy and disruptive to the musical line, and he looks physically uncomfortable as well. When asked what he knows about breath control, he responds, "It's something about supporting from the diaphragm, but I don't really understand it."

What causes confusion about breathing, and how can we lead our students to a clear understanding of this all-important function? In my view, it's the use of those two words "diaphragmatic support." This term is vague and misleading, and makes younger players feel that breathing—which needs to be viewed as a very natural process—is somehow mysterious.

Anatomically speaking, the diaphragm is a membranous partition that separates the abdominal cavity from the chest cavity and is attached to the lower ribs and lumbar spine. It is an unusual muscle because it is both involuntary and voluntary. When you aren't thinking about it, the diaphragm regulates the speed of respiration to suit the amount of bodily activity. But you can also speed up and slow down diaphragmatic action at will. Most important to remember is that it works in only *one* phase of breathing: inhalation. As it drops, air rushes into the lungs to fill the vacuum created by the diaphragm's action. Once the lungs are filled, other muscles are involved in controlling exhalation—namely the abdominals and intercostals, which lie between the ribs. Helping a young wind player to feel an easeful expansion and

15

contraction of these muscles can be a major challenge, because many students (and professionals) mistakenly believe that abdominal tightness is necessary for good breath control.

On the contrary! If I allow my abdominals to become rigid while playing a phrase, I'm in deep trouble whenever I need to replenish my air supply, especially if there is time for only a quick snatch breath. Equating tightness with "support" can have negative, if not disastrous, consequences for all wind players, since tension in the abdominals can constrict the diaphragm's action and reduce the amount of breath inhaled. Furthermore, since tension in one area of the body generally leads to tension in other areas, a struggle to inhale deeply soon becomes a battle to maintain an open throat and relaxed back, neck, shoulders, arms, and hands. Learning to guide the air stream energetically and steadily while avoiding tension in the muscles of exhalation should be every wind player's goal.

To convince players that tense abdominals limit their breath capacity, try this effective series of exercises, designed by James Kortum of the Sydney Conservatorium flute faculty.

1. Without your instrument, tighten the abdominal muscles by pulling in your stomach. Remember that the abdominals are a sheath of muscles extending from the abdomen up to the ribs—as anyone who has ever done sit-ups or "crunches" can attest!
2. Maintaining this muscular tension, inhale and begin to expel air slowly from your mouth, as if gently blowing out a candle.
3. Still keeping the abdominals contracted, inhale and repeat this cycle two more times. Ask yourself if this unpleasantly tense sensation is similar to how you feel when playing the end of a long phrase, and if your subsequent breaths are fully satisfying or constricted.
4. Begin the next exercise as in steps 1 and 2, keeping the abdominals tight. After exhaling for about three seconds, release the abdominal tension and continue to blow, meanwhile maintaining the same airspeed.
5. Repeat this cycle twice, always beginning with contracted abdominals and then softening the muscles during exhalation. At this point, ask yourself if there is a noticeable difference in your breath capacity when you exhale with relaxed abdominals.
6. Still without your instrument, inhale with tight abdominals, begin to exhale, relax the abdominals, and when your air supply is depleted, allow air to enter your body naturally, in its own rhythm.
7. Repeat this cycle two more times, *but with relaxed abdominals* at all times. Are you now starting to sense a natural rhythm to your breathing, perhaps even a slight pause between exhalation and inhalation? Are you becoming more aware of abdominal tension?

After completing these exercises without your instrument, repeat them while playing a scale in whole notes in a comfortable register. Ask yourself the same questions once again, and pay special attention to the quality of sound produced when abdominals are clenched. There will be a noticeable difference, especially in notes following an inhalation.

Since the action of the abdominals is sometimes misconstrued as being "diaphragmatic," many wind players tend to think solely about expanding below the waistline when inhaling. Focusing exclusively on the abdominals neglects the vitally important expansion and contraction of the intercostals.

Singers utilize the entire torso—abdominal cavity and ribs—when breathing. Unbeknownst to many people, the top rib actually lies slightly above the clavicle (collar bone), a fact that should help students to understand what a large portion of the torso our ribs occupy. We also need to remember that the diaphragm and the lungs, which are approximately football-sized when fully inflated, are located higher in our chests than we might realize. As the diaphragm drops, it helps the lower ribs to rise and expand at the end of inhalation. At the end of an exhalation, the ribs naturally descend, helping the diaphragm to rise and return to its highest domed position. Interfering with this natural action denies us the full benefit that our breathing mechanism is designed to offer.

Showing a DVD of a great singer such as Cecilia Bartoli would certainly be an excellent way to convince young wind players to pay more attention to the intercostal muscles' role in breathing. In addition, a simple demonstration requiring no equipment whatsoever is to have students sit comfortably in a chair, feet flat on the floor, directly under the knees and hip width apart. Ask them to lean forward and rest their chests comfortably on their thighs, letting their heads hang over their knees. Next tell them to take a few slow, deep breaths and then ask what they observed. Expansion of the rib cage (in back as well as in front) is extremely easy to feel in this position, which also demonstrates how the shoulders naturally stay relaxed throughout a breath cycle. Tense shoulders in wind playing can cause throat constriction and wreak havoc with the quality of sound being produced; if you notice tense shoulders in a student, gently encourage the idea of the head floating upwards, balanced atop a free, flexible neck that is connected to a long, wide back. Remind students that they also can sense the impressive expansion of the ribs—especially to the sides—whenever they lie on their backs, breathing normally.

Encourage your young wind players to allow their sternums (breastbones) to rise when inhaling; paying attention to this area of the chest will improve both posture and breath capacity. Keeping the sternum high (rather than slouching) assures that lungs are extended to their full length. This in turn creates lower internal air pressure, and results in a more natural inhalation as air rushes to enter the body and fill the awaiting vacuum in the lungs.

Although preoccupation with just one area of the torso while breathing can impede the development of total breath control, encourage students to focus their attention temporarily on the area that is least natural for them to expand. Each human body is somewhat different from the next, and among your students there will be great variety in rib cage width, distance between the lower ribs and pelvis, and inclination to hold tension. As students begin to sense the combined action of abdominals, intercostals, and the upper chest, suggest that they take luxuriously slow breaths, out of tempo, while practicing an etude or solo. This practice technique will help them to feel what they are aiming to accomplish when breathing quickly in a musical context.

One final thought. As we work to improve our students' comprehension of breathing and their ability to breathe, we are well served by describing the breath as our bow. Just as an accomplished string player can define a musical gesture through masterful, well-considered bowing, we wind players can bring life to a phrase through easeful and intelligent breathing. Long legato lines, ringing staccato notes, and fluent tongued passages are best produced with an air stream that is guided by a firm yet flexible musculature. Stiffness and tension will sabotage our best intentions, whereas breathing as naturally as if we were speaking or singing unselfconsciously will allow us to forge a powerful bond with our listeners. Demystify breathing and the reward will be more communicative, joyful music making. ➙

The Art of Practice

Mary Karen Clardy

Musical achievement flows naturally from daily practice of the building blocks of music, scales, and arpeggios. The foundation of simple melodies or virtuoso technical passages, scales are the framework for learning repertoire, developing confidence, and communicating musical phrasing to the audience. With both the internal and external ears engaged, practice prepares a flutist to interpret phrasing, reducing practice time and rewarding the audience with a higher quality of musical artistry. In addition to the standard exercises of Altès, Barrère, Maquarre, or Taffanel-Gaubert, flutists benefit from creating new routines based on technical challenges of orchestral excerpts or solo repertoire.

INGREDIENTS:
Organized study increases learning efficiency, and this step should always precede a first reading of new music. First determine key/tonality and meter, visually identifying repeated melodic or rhythmic patterns; then practice difficulties by verbalizing rhythms, saying note names aloud, and fingering awkward patterns. By adding these simple steps, preparation begins before the first note sounds, saving time and energy in practice.

The old adage that practice makes perfect is particularly important in order to develop muscle memory. Isolate rhythmic and technical challenges, then practice in repetitions of 5–10 units, maintaining accurate rhythmic proportion at a slower tempo. Metronome use reveals inaccuracies, such as rushing, dragging, or hesitation in practice, and monitors the small tempo fluctuations that affect musical flow. Create variations to maintain concentration in a practice session by always engaging the mind. Examples include altering rhythms by changing to dotted or triplet patterns, playing up or down an octave from the written notes, reversing the order of the pitches, or multiple tonguing (either double or triple tongue) the printed notes in a difficult pattern. The variations are unlimited, so be creative!

Begin practice sessions at different starting points in order to build confidence throughout a long work, for example begin at the end or middle of the piece. Optimum concentration occurs at the beginning of practice, and varying the location at the start of a session allows the flutist to distribute mental energy from beginning to end. Another helpful technique for audition preparation is to practice at different times of day in order to increase mental and physical flexibility. After setting program order for a concert, it's also helpful to change practice order of the works frequently to ensure equal preparation time.

Always engage the mind and internal ear, avoiding repetitive practice, which encourages bad musical and technical habits. Body tension occurs when fingers are unprepared for note changes, and issues of muscle tension/tendinitis/overuse syndrome result from this type of practice. Smooth technical flow develops from internally hearing pitches before playing aloud, and daily scale studies provide the opportunity to establish smooth phrasing throughout difficult technical passages. Memorizing music eliminates reliance on the printed page, and daily technical routines should be played from memory to develop ear training and musical phrasing. Freedom from the printed page allows the flutist to explore tone color, dynamics, phrase direction, and often improves breath control.

A daily practice routine develops consistency in learning and the muscular strength necessary for good physical health and longevity as a flutist. A minimum of 30 minutes to 1 hour a day should be spent with scales, arpeggios, or other exercises that focus on ear training, scale study, and technical development. Shorter practice sessions are particularly important for young flutists in order to maintain concentration and avoid fatigue in embouchure and in hand and arm muscles. Even throughout a flutist's career, 5 to 10 minutes of focused practice is the best way to correct habits or learn new techniques.

SERVES:

This recipe builds practice skills for every flutist, from beginner through professional, in order to increase confidence in performance. Efficient practice is the simultaneous process of building technical consistency and developing musical line, so investigate creative solutions to optimize practice sessions. Remember that playing through music is never the best way to prepare, and that thorough practice at a slow tempo develops both technical and musical aspects. At every opportunity, attend live concerts to experience the connection between musical phrasing, technical command, stage presence, and communication, and always remember that quality practice is behind every artistic performance. ➤●

Recipe for Preventing Playing-Related Health Problems

William J. Dawson, M.D.

INGREDIENTS:
Knowing why problems occur
Knowing what problems occur
Knowing how to detect problems
A pinch of basic body structure and function
Logic and common sense to figure out prevention strategies

SERVES:
All woodwind musicians—performers, teachers, and students.

PREPARATION:
Playing-related problems are common—a 1986 survey of more than 2,200 symphony and opera musicians found that 76 percent had 1 or more problems severe enough to affect their performance. Females had more than males, 84 percent to 72 percent. The highest prevalence was for musculoskeletal difficulties, with 58 percent describing one or more problems overall. This latter group had a 66 percent prevalence for strings, 48 percent for woodwinds, and 60 percent for other instruments. About half the males complained of musculoskeletal problems, and 70 percent of females; women were especially vulnerable as the size of their instrument increased.

For the musician, the greatest concern relates to hand and upper extremity problems. This is particularly true for the young instrumentalist, working hard and long to train and develop a career. Adding a bit of common sense to these facts, it's important for both old and young musicians and their teachers to learn how to recognize and prevent these problems.

Why?
The most common difficulties are caused by physical *overuse*—a practice or activity in which parts of the body have been used in a so-called normal manner, but to an extent that has exceeded their biological limits and thereby produced certain physical changes. It can occur with playing music as well as a wide variety of occupations and other activities. Individuals vary in susceptibility to developing problems from overuse.

The causes and contributing factors in overuse are related to changes in *time x intensity* of playing, technique errors, and genetic factors. Most common in the first category are rapid changes in activity without time for the body to compensate. Examples include a new school/

instructor/employer/instrument/repertoire/performing organization/environment/management. Other factors include learning additional instruments, increased practice time or altered practice schedule prior to juries, recitals, auditions, or concerts. Overuse is common when returning to school in the fall after a musically less active summer.

Improper playing techniques (some call this *misuse*) include abnormal body postures, excessive pressure or force on keys or strings, a physical mismatch between player and instrument (think of a ten-year old trying to play baritone saxophone), and using too many muscles (more on this later).

Genetic causes include hypermobility, or lax ligaments, a congenital condition present in 5 to 8 percent of young musicians, especially girls. Joints can move in wider ranges than normal, affecting playing techniques.

What?

Here is a basic list of physical conditions brought on by overuse, from the most common to the least:

1. *Muscle strain*, especially of the wrist and forearm (both sides), the small muscles of the hand, and often the shoulder and spine. These usually are caused by excessive force and/or repetition.
2. *Inflammation* on and around tendons, mostly around the wrist, in the palm, and at the elbows, again from repetitive movements or direct pressure.
3. *Joint irritation* and inflammation, produced from excessive motion or stretch of tissues surrounding the joint, or by repetitive, forceful compression across joint surfaces.
4. *Nerve compression* problems, particularly carpal tunnel syndrome at the wrist.

How?

Detecting these problems means knowing what to look for (in medical terms, these are *symptoms* and *signs*). By far the most common and important symptom is *pain*. It comes from pressure on the belly of the muscle, at its bony origin or insertion, and/or at the junction of muscle and tendon. Pain also may occur with active muscle contraction or passive muscle stretch. Tendons often are painful too, especially in the hand and wrist; the musician may feel thickening, or perhaps a rubbing sensation. These symptoms usually are noticed after repetitive movements or direct pressure on the overused structure. Some musicians may complain of pain in neck, shoulders, or middle- or lower-back muscles, which often is worse with movement.

Other symptoms may include feelings of tightness, stiffness, weakness, tiredness, heaviness, cramping, or warmth. Pain can occur around a joint, and may be worse with movement or stretch. Nerve compression symptoms include clumsiness, decreased coordination, loss of finger or tongue speed, numbness, and tingling.

Now, mix together our new knowledge in order to find ways to prevent problems. The three most important bits of knowledge are:

1. The mechanisms and contributing factors that cause playing-related problems.
2. Basics of our own body structure and function (also known as anatomy and physiology).
3. Some ergonomic and biomechanical principles of correct playing.

Let's begin with a suggestion that applies to all instrumentalists: lower the *time x intensity* product in playing by practicing 25 minutes of every half hour, then resting the other 5. Get away from the instrument; do something unrelated. When increased playing is inevitable, make changes gradually, not abruptly. If that's not possible, try to do shorter sessions with more rest between.

Next, being in balance physically can prevent many problems. In this kind of balance, muscle tension is at a minimum, and opposing groups of muscles are not fighting each other. Movement away from resting posture requires fewer muscles and less power. This is especially important for our hands.

Playing relaxed uses the principles of being in balance. Correct holding and playing posture can be efficient (using only the muscles and force needed), or tense (using too many muscles or too much force, or contracting both sets of opposing muscles simultaneously). Once you have assumed the correct posture, bring the instrument to you. Keep your upper extremities as close as possible to their resting position, adjusting only if necessary, and hold the instrument by using the fewest possible muscles. Let the shoulders hang loosely and naturally. All this posture work also provides an improved spinal alignment, with the additional benefit of more efficient breathing. Work to keep your neck and throat muscles relaxed; not only can this lessen the possibility of overuse, it also helps produce a fuller tone.

External instrument supports are mandatory for some woodwind instruments, but may be very helpful for others as well. They relieve muscles of unnecessary tension and work effort, and can improve playing tone and endurance. The choice of support depends on individual capabilities, needs, playing style, and the type of instrument played.

Seeing what you need to see is also crucial. Sightlines to both the music and the conductor must be correct, and not stress the neck and shoulder muscles. Poor posture may result from poor vision (do you need glasses?). The "mature" musician may require correction of *presbyopia* for seeing the music as well as working with reeds.

Music teachers can play a major role in preventing problems in their students. Technical factors in overuse are most often postural or positional, so the teacher should look for them, tell the student, and modify the situation. Playing relaxed is great advice for this group also. It doesn't come naturally, and must be taught for most pupils. Teachers can also identify hypermobility (double-jointedness) and encourage proper positioning of joints. Sometimes musical exercises to help strengthen muscles can help to control inefficient joint motions and improve playing facility.

Teachers should also be careful in changing technique of a student who is new to them. It's best if problem items are addressed and changed one at a time. Add new techniques and music slowly, as the student's comfort permits. Finally, accept the long-term nature of developing new habits and incorporating them into routines, musical and otherwise. ➝●

Whistle While You Play

Doris DeLoach

INGREDIENTS:
Air, lips, and a responsive oboe reed

SERVES:
Oboists yearning to improve endurance, intonation, tone, and flexibility.

A prevalent problem of oboists is that we use too much lip pressure and not enough air. Sometimes that results from using a reed that is simply too hard, too flat, or even too easy. We can blow and blow, but unless the embouchure allows the air to pass through the reed, blowing more without the proper embouchure and/or reed can increase tension and make us feel and sound even worse. In order to be able to use a **generous** amount of air, we must have a **responsive reed** that has the correct amount of resistance and **no flatness** in pitch, and we must work for a **permissive** and flexible embouchure. Often, a reed that is too easy encourages biting, in order to hold the pitch up or to keep the tone from being an embarrassment.

The reed is of paramount importance in learning to blow properly and to form the embouchure correctly, but the following recipe is based on the assumption that the reed is responsive and has been made to play as closely in tune as possible (with a "c" crow). The reed must be one that encourages the player to open the embouchure rather than to close the embouchure. This kind of reed allows playing toward the tip of the reed with no biting or squeezing the reed from top to bottom. The embouchure must be **permissive**, *not* coercive. We must **allow** the reed to vibrate instead of coercing the reed to vibrate.

Practice making the embouchure with the reed alone:

Form the embouchure just as you would whistle. The corners of the mouth come forward, the chin goes downward, and the flesh on the chin assumes the structure of the chin (the flesh does not bunch up). The jaw teeth open as the corners of the lips are pulled forward and inward and as the lips form a whistle.

Hold the reed with your thumb underneath the cork, your index finger on top of the thread and the tip of the reed placed in the center of the red of the lower lip. A small amount of friction exists between the lower lip and the reed because the reed, at approximately a 45-degree angle to the head, presses slightly downward into the lower lip. (The holding position of the thumb and index finger assists in this; it is similar to holding the oboe with the right thumb under the thumb rest and the left index finger on the B key.) The lips and the reed, moving together, are then rolled in to the point of a "stalemate"—that is, a point where the lips won't go in any further (the pulling downward of the chin is very important—it is that structure which does not allow the entire lower lip to roll into the mouth). The lips maintain the whistle-like shape. It is normal for the oboe reed to continually want to slide inward. It is important that the reed begins in the proper position and that it does not move independently of the lower lip. **Avoid** allowing the reed to go into the mouth **without** the lips going with it by thinking of the lips as continually saying to the reed, *"Nu, nu, you can't come in."*

Exercises for lip flexibility and reed placement:

1. Smile-pucker-smile-pucker saying "eee-uuu-eee-uuu" with the **tip** of the reed placed on the center of the lower lip. You will notice that the pitch changes from higher with the smile/eee to lower with the pucker/uuu.
2. Form the whistle embouchure with the **tip** of the reed placed on the center of the lower lip. Open and close the jaw as in chewing. You will notice that the pitch changes very little but the timbre of the sound changes as the mouth cavity opens and closes.
3. On the reed alone, practice playing a chromatic scale from C down to G and then from G up to C by rolling the reed and lip in and out.

When blowing, use a generous amount of air. Produce a robust tone with no hint of pinching in the quality. These exercises should be practiced regularly before placing the reed in the oboe. These exercises will help the embouchure to be mobile. This kind of flexibility assists in changing timbre and dynamics and improving intonation. ➤●

The Clarinet Makeover: Successful Basics of Jaw and Tongue Position Can Quickly and Easily Solve Three of Your Students' Most Prevalent Clarinet Problems

Julie DeRoche

All good teachers have tried to solve the problems experienced by many young clarinet players, of undertone while trying to achieve high notes, puffy cheeks, and noisy and ungraceful or "twangy" articulation. The solution to these problems is finding the correct jaw and tongue positions. Following this recipe for successful position of jaw and tongue will produce a successful player and happy teacher.

INGREDIENTS:
Flexible and willing clarinet students, teachers with direct, easy to follow information, and some instruction time.

SERVES:
This recipe serves any clarinet player facing difficulties with undertone in the upper register, inconsistency of tone and pitch, puffy cheeks, and rough articulation. It also serves teachers looking for solutions to these problems.

Undertone
Do your students have difficulty playing high notes, instead creating a barking or low groaning sound? When trying for their high notes, have you seen them squeeze their eyes shut and grip the mouthpiece between their teeth until their lips hurt? The reason for this is that they are using the jaw (meaning the jawbone itself—not the chin muscle) in a completely incorrect way. The secret ingredient for solving this problem is correct jaw position: *The jaw must move forward rather than upward.*

To solve the undertone problem, try this yourself. Begin by opening your mouth so that the teeth are approximately 1 centimeter apart. Gently move the lower jaw very slightly forward so that the bottom teeth are almost parallel or "lined up" with the upper teeth. This position of the jaw allows for good control of the reed in a forward direction rather than an upward direction, is a key factor in avoiding biting, and makes problems of undertone disappear. In fact, it actually opens the bite slightly, maintaining control of the sound without pinching or cutting off vibration of the reed. Be sure to open the mouth the correct distance, (1 centimeter) which will allow you to set the top teeth on the top of the mouthpiece approximately ¼ inch from the tip of the mouthpiece, and the "pressure point" or lower lip and

even teeth like flute

teeth approximately ½ inch from the tip of the reed. It is important that you do not open the mouth too wide.

When you place the mouthpiece in your mouth, apply some upward pressure of the two hands toward the top teeth so that the weight of the clarinet does not rest on the lower half of the embouchure. This will help you to maintain firm, comfortable control of the sound without lower lip injury or bite.

Remember, move the jaw slightly forward. While doing this, roll the lower lip into the mouth, and pull the chin muscle flat against the jawbone. You will now have a leverage of "lip in, chin down, and jaw forward." Next, pull the corners of the lips in toward the "canine" teeth. They will be directed toward the sides of the mouthpiece when the mouthpiece is placed in the mouth. Last, but definitely not least, the top lip will also be held tightly against the teeth and will move downward toward the mouthpiece. The combination of the correct jaw position, combined with improved muscle position in chin, corners and top lip, will create beautiful, clear tone in all registers.

As an experiment, play (or ask your student to play) a scale, moving up to the highest successful note, and then further to the first unsuccessful note—the one with the undertone. As you attempt this note, remember to continue to move the jaw forward to the reed until the undertone disappears. This is where you should place the jaw at all times. Finding this position, and learning to hold it for the entire range, will improve overall tone, make the high notes respond, alleviate biting, and alter pitch in a positive way. And most important— undertone disappears forever.

Puffy Cheeks

Most students know that they are not supposed to puff their cheeks. However, they have a hard time fixing the problem, because they logically think that the solution involves the cheeks. It doesn't! *The way to stop puffy cheeks is to correct the tongue position.*

Since the cheeks are (for the most part) tissue rather than muscle, your student will not be able to voluntarily stop puffing the cheeks with the cheeks. What is it that causes this problem?

Without the clarinet in hand, try blowing air out of your mouth with the tongue in a low or open position—in other words, push it down. It doesn't have to be much. Any pushing of the tongue in a downward direction will cause the air to stray to the cheeks and push them in an outward direction. The cheeks will puff because the tongue is too low and the air is flowing sideways rather than forward. (This is a good reason never to say, "Open your throat" to a clarinet player. Opening the throat actually causes the player to push the tongue down, creating bad tone, flat pitch, and puffy cheeks.)

Now try saying the word "shhh." Yes—just like you are telling someone to be quiet. In this position, the tongue is relaxed and high in the mouth, the tip of the tongue is just behind the front teeth, and the air is directed forward. Next, try blowing very hard with the tongue in this position—a loud, fast-moving "*Shhhhhh!*" No matter the speed of the air, *the cheeks do not puff.* Since the tongue is relaxed and high in the mouth, the air does not move sideways and the cheeks are not forced in an outward direction.

Now try playing the clarinet with the tongue in this position. Do not let yourself push the tongue down or move it backward in the mouth. Blow air forward to the reed while thinking the syllable, "shhh." The pitch and tone will be more consistent, because the oral cavity is

Don't say "open throat"

26

more consistently shaped. The reed will respond more clearly and quickly because the air is directed forward, right to it. The cheeks will not puff—in fact, cannot puff—and the problem is solved.

Noisy, Twangy Articulation

Now that the jaw is correct, the undertone is gone, and the air column is focused by the "shhh" tongue position so that the cheeks do not puff, it is easy to articulate clearly, consistently, with good tone and good pitch. The secret is to move the tongue only slightly, only at the tip, and *with the syllable "tee" rather than "tah."*

To learn how to accomplish this, first practice articulation motion without the clarinet. Close your mouth and think about the position of your tongue while it is at rest. It is most likely lying along the roof of your mouth, and the "tip of the top" of the tongue is resting gently behind your front teeth. This is the tongue's natural and relaxed position—very much as it is when blowing with the syllable "shhh." Now open your mouth slightly, keeping your tongue relaxed and high, and do not alter the forward or backward position of the tongue. Inhale, and then replace the tip of your tongue on the roof of your mouth (or gum line) just behind the front teeth. Think the word "tee." Let go of the air, or blow, while "saying" this syllable. However, do not actually use the vocal chords. Merely blow the tongue off of the roof of your mouth, lightly, and without any tension or force of the tongue. Let the air do the majority of the work.

Repeat this action (tee, tee, tee) until you are sure that you are moving only the tip of your tongue. Most of your tongue remains stationary, and the tip of the tongue moves in a small downward motion. Be sure to articulate this syllable off of the gum line behind your top teeth. Do not allow your tongue to touch the back of your top or bottom teeth or your bottom lip. Remember, this is for practice without the clarinet, and will change slightly when you add the clarinet to the picture.

Now try to repeat this motion while playing your clarinet. When you place the mouthpiece in your mouth, the tip of the reed will be just behind your top teeth, in almost exactly the same place as described above, near your gum line. However, *instead of moving the tongue off of the roof of your mouth, you will instead move it off of the reed.* Inhale. Touch the reed with the "tip of the top" of your tongue, very slightly below the tip or top edge of the reed. Think the syllable "tee." Using the exact same motion that you used while practicing without the clarinet, remove your tongue from the tip of the reed. When you release the reed, release your air. If you have taken a good breath, your reed will vibrate the very second it is released. When you want it to stop again, merely return the tongue to the exact position from which you just removed it. You do not have to *push* the reed in order to stop it. Since you are now articulating at the thinnest point of your reed, you may merely touch it and it will stop.

Remember, we want a consistent oral cavity in order to keep consistent tone and pitch. Using the tee syllable helps keep the majority of the tongue stationary, thereby keeping the oral cavity from changing at every articulation, and in turn, keeps the tone and pitch consistent—no twang. Further, the light touch reduces noise, the directed air makes quick response, and the tongue can develop speed, because the reduced motion makes it more efficient.

Learning Time

Of course, all of these techniques take practice, and often, some undoing of prior learned problems. But with clear and easy ingredients for teaching the correct methods, problems can be solved, and you can achieve your clarinet makeover. After working on this recipe for success, your students will find that playing clarinet is easier than they thought it was, problems that you thought were almost unsolvable will disappear, and you will have a clarinet section that is everything you hoped it would be.

Spice Up Your Ensemble with a Dash of Bassoon—A Recipe for Supporting and Encouraging Young Bassoonists

William Dietz

Just as you may plant herbs and spices in your garden for your specialty dishes, in the same way you must plant and nurture your young bassoonists. Sprinkle liberally on your ensemble for a rich flavor. Give young bassoonists plenty of attention and a private teacher (expert gardener), time to grow (plant early, but remember the growing season is year round), the best equipment you can afford (choose ingredients carefully), and lots of opportunities to perform (simmer with gentle but constant heat).

INGREDIENTS:
Motivated young bassoonists and supportive music directors

SERVES:
Initial serving for the young bassoonist. Subsequent unlimited servings provide for all who will collaborate with the maturing bassoonist.

I. The Problem
Very often, precollege bassoon players in an ensemble are not at a comparable level to their peers in other sections of the band. As a judge for all-state and regional bands and orchestras over the past twenty-five years, I often hear young bassoonists who haven't begun to wrestle with some of the basics of intermediate/advanced bassoon playing such as tenor clef reading, reed adjustment, and vibrato production. Often they have a limited technical level on the instrument. When you consider that many are self-taught, and only play their instruments about a third of the year (when you factor in summer and marching season), this is not surprising. Here are some strategies for helping your bassoon players stay connected to their instruments year round.

II. The Use of Instrument in Exchange for Private Study Contract
If your ensemble program is supplying the instrument to the young bassoonist, a convincing argument can be made that its use should be reserved for someone who agrees to study privately. Think of it this way; the instrument belongs to *all* the members of the ensemble and its use (or misuse) will affect the musical experience of every member of the group. Clearly, many works that are at the core of the repertoire have critical parts for the bassoon and can't be performed without them, but just as importantly, all members of the ensemble deserve the opportunity to see and hear the bassoon as part of their music education.

Bassoons are among the most costly instruments. Even at the student level, instruments can cost several thousand dollars. Often an ensemble will own only one or two bassoons. If seems only fair to expect that the student chosen to use the instrument will "pay back" for the use of this instrument by studying privately and thus utilizing the instruments to its potential. A spirit of giving back for the good of the ensemble makes sense and should be encouraged. When a band/orchestra director chooses someone from a larger woodwind section to switch to the bassoon, this strategy should be considered.

Bassoon study should be done year round, not just during the concert season and should not stop during the summer months. (Special encouragement should be given to the bassoonist to participate in summer music camps. There are even camps that specialize in reed making.) Imagine how difficult it is to progress if you put your instrument away in June and start up again the following January! It goes without saying that having a private, expert teacher solves many of the unique issues of bassoon playing, such as reed and instrument adjustments and the specialized techniques, such as flicking and half hole. A private teacher relieves some of this responsibility from the music director.

III. Chamber Music

If your school does not have an orchestra that includes wind players and/or if there is not a concert wind ensemble during the fall term, the double reed players may have no performance outlet. Perhaps they are playing another instrument during the marching band season. Small ensemble practice that uses bassoon (such as wind quintet, quartet, or trio) is an excellent win/win strategy that keeps the bassoonist playing and progressing.

There are two main problems with running small ensembles of this type: dearth of appropriate repertoire and time commitment from the music director. However the pluses for the bassoonist (and other players) are substantial. They will stay connected to the bassoon during a period when they normally may not be playing. In addition their musical skills will improve enormously from participation in chamber music (something that ultimately helps the large ensemble.) Finally they may find an extremely enjoyable outlet for music making.

The problem of appropriate repertoire is a real one. Much standard material for small ensembles is generally too difficult for junior/senior high school players of mixed abilities. However there is a small body of works that is very appropriate to this level and can be a lot of fun to play. Lists of graded repertoire are available from many sources. Suggestions from local professional players and arrangements of popular, folk, and light classics can provide the momentum the ensemble needs. After a few seasons of small ensemble work, the music director can develop a library of appropriate materials that can be repeated as the ensemble personnel changes.

The second problem is one of time commitment from the music director. Often small ensembles need to rehearse before or after school, and band/orchestra directors have very little time for extra rehearsals. I have found that often students are motivated to rehearse without constant supervision. Actually some musical skills seem to improve if the students are left alone and forced to think for themselves. However the music director is critical, especially at the beginning rehearsals, to show the students how to rehearse. Afterwards the music director should check in from time to time to make sure that things are progressing well and to provide coaching sessions.

This ensemble does not necessarily have to have a performance as a goal, but this is certainly an incentive. An end-of-the-semester informal concert for friends during band period is often enough to motivate an ensemble to practice.

The bassoon is an instrument with a wide range of possibilities. It can spice up your ensemble but requires a little bit of a "hothouse approach" to grow to fruition. The results in your ensemble sauce can be well worth the effort. ━●

Successful Show Performance

Mike Duva

INGREDIENTS:
Equipment, time management, mental preparation, proper ATTITUDE!

SERVES:
Those musicians who have the occasion to perform in a show (whether it be a one-night celebrity act or an extended production show).

A successful show performance is defined, in my opinion, as the completion of a show with the knowledge that you have done the job to the best of your ability and your employer is pleased with the result.

Many factors contribute to a successful performance, a few of which were not taught in school when I was in attendance. Several items that I will mention are simply common sense.

1. Equipment

As a woodwind player, I have been fortunate enough to acquire the instruments necessary to keep myself employable. These would be soprano, alto, tenor, and baritone saxophone, clarinet and bass clarinet, piccolo, flute, and alto and bass flute. Many doublers also include oboe, English horn, and bassoon in their personal "arsenals," making themselves that much more employable. In my experience I have found that the basic instruments needed by a doubler are alto and tenor sax, piccolo, flute, and clarinet. Having started as a "low reed" player, I was expected to play baritone and tenor sax, clarinet, bass clarinet, piccolo, and flute. The obvious assumption is that the individual is proficient on said instruments. Make certain that you have all of the necessary accessories (reeds, instrument stands, pencils, etc.) to facilitate a successful performance. To state the obvious, proper attire is a must; a black tuxedo (men) or black formal wear (women) is the norm (not, as I have actually seen, a blue or purple tux jacket!).

2. Time Management

Simply stated, be on time for the rehearsal and the show. At the appointed time, every musician should be ready to start playing, not walking in the door or setting up equipment. In addition to being very poor etiquette, not being on time is extremely disrespectful to your fellow musicians. I have experienced rehearsals in which musicians have arrived a minute or two after the scheduled start time, the result being that they were not called again for a show. To quote Dr. Tim Lautzenheiser (former instructor of mine), "To be on time is to be late; to be early is to be on time." I have never forgotten that piece of wisdom and common sense. This is the easiest of the ingredients to digest!

3. Mental Preparation

This aspect of performance can, in many ways, be the most difficult. You need to be focused on the situation at hand. Leave your personal "issues" at the stage door; you have a job to do.

Good sight-reading is an absolute must; hopefully, one has practiced that invaluable skill. Fortunately, my former teachers (especially Chuck West) insisted on playing duets in every lesson. It cannot be stressed enough what an important this tool is.

A musical director for a celebrity act is there to conduct the band or orchestra, not to show an individual how to play a certain passage.

We must remember, also, to pay strict attention to the music at hand and the conductor, not the act. On the several occasions that I have worked with the Temptations, it is very difficult not to watch the amazing choreography that these gentlemen perform. But I am not there to watch their performance; I am there, along with the rest of the band, to add to their performance.

Pete Brewer, a prominent woodwind player in the Dallas/Fort Worth, Texas area, gave me one of the best pieces of advice that I ever received with regard to show playing. When I asked him for any suggestions he might have for me with regard to working shows, he responded with, "Keep your eyes and ears open, and your mouth shut!" That has been of benefit to me many times as well.

Occasionally, an improvised solo may be required during the course of a show. The solo should be played in the style of the artist or the genre. This is one example of when your music listening habits and practice come to fruition. Example: On one occasion when I was with the Glenn Miller Orchestra, I had just hired a new tenor sax player who was to play the solo on Miller's classic version of "Stardust," which began with a two-measure solo break. This young man, instead of staying within the "Miller style," played that break in an avant-garde style that I will never forget! Needless to say, after the show he received a lecture from the bandleader.

On a more recent occasion, I performed with the Coasters ("Yakety Yak," "Charlie Brown"). During the rehearsal, the musical director realized that the solo tenor sax part (which is an integral part of the song) for "Charlie Brown" was not in the book, so he told me to "fake it." I had heard and played that tune many times before and had made a conscious effort to retain it, therefore enabling me to do an acceptable job for him.

4. Proper Attitude

I have found that when I am in a new show performance situation, the gig usually goes well the first one or two times. This might be attributed to the fact that everything is new and you have to really concentrate to "stay on top" of the music. The proverbial "edge" that you feel in a new performance is extremely helpful in keeping the music fresh and alive. After the "newness" of the performance erodes (very quickly, I might add), the performance can become stagnant, leading to a lack of concentration that can lead to mistakes. I work a six-night-per-week production show on a regular basis and it can be very hard to keep the same music fresh night after night. In my attempt at maintaining the proper attitude, I look for ways to keep the show interesting, whether it be watching the audience's reactions to the music or keeping in touch musically with the other band members while on stage.

For all musicians, a positive attitude is an extremely desirable quality to possess.

Improved Intonation for Young Clarinetists

Clark W Fobes

INGREDIENTS:
A small mirror
Candle and lighter
A pinch of patience

SERVES:
Clarinetists and their directors and teachers.

Proper intonation for young students is a problem that is very often ignored in the hopes that "it will eventually get better." I believe that good intonation can be learned and taught fairly early. Without getting into a long pedagogical discussion about acoustics and hearing, I would like to delineate a few basic tips that I have found work well with young students.

Most young students tend to play flat. It is a function of learning to use muscles in an unfamiliar way. I don't worry about flat pitch in the first few weeks or even months, but as muscles firm up and the student becomes familiar with playing and holding the clarinet, he/she should be able to achieve good basic intonation.

Intonation is always a function of good **tone production**. The primary focus of this article will be the elements of clarinet tone: the **mouthpiece**, the **embouchure**, **breath support**, and **physical support of the clarinet.** Of course, one cannot begin to attempt to teach a clarinetist if he/she does not have a good clarinet in good repair.

Before considering the physiological elements of producing a good tone the student **must** have a good **mouthpiece**. The mouthpiece and reed are the basic tone-generating system of the clarinet and the ***fundamental variable*** for proper intonation other than the player. The mouthpiece should be of a medium close design and students should **not** play a reed softer than a Vandoren number 2 1/2. The mouthpiece should respond easily with a good focus. The **CLARK W FOBES *Debut*** mouthpiece is designed specifically in this manner. I recommend that students move up to a number 3 strength reed as soon as possible.

After the mouthpiece, the **embouchure** is the next greatest variable in tone production. Correct embouchure is a tricky concept to teach and may take several weeks for a student to achieve. Here is the method I teach, which produces a good embouchure for most students at the first lesson:

Assuming that you have already gone over the fundamentals of the position of the mouthpiece in the mouth and the student can produce an "E" (first finger and thumb), ask him/her to remove the clarinet from their mouth. Have them look into a mirror and say "oo" and hold the shape of their lips. Now ask them to say "ee" without moving their lips from the "oo" position. They will not be able to do it, but what you want them to do is hold the "oo" shape with a slight pulling in the corners. This also puts a nice dip in the chin just below the lower lip. The sound "oo" also places the oral cavity in a good position for proper air flow. "O" or "ah" opens the throat too much and causes a flattening of pitch. For this reason I also teach the syllable "t-oo" for tonguing.

Once the student can produce this shape without the clarinet, try again with the clarinet in the mouth. **ALWAYS USE A MIRROR**. I find that students are still very visually oriented at this point and their own model is best for visualization. Most students will be able to do this in the first lesson, but it is very important to keep hounding them on good embouchure every week.

Proper **breath support** is fundamental to getting the reed to vibrate at a sufficient speed to produce good tone and pitch. I cringe whenever I hear an educator using the old saw, "*Support with the diaphragm!*" In fact, the diaphragm has nothing to do with support and everything to do with breathing **in.** The diaphragm is a dome-shaped muscle below the plural cavity that can **only pull downwards** and is not involved in **pushing** air out. Diaphragmatic breathing is what we all do naturally. What we want to teach is how to breathe in **efficiently** and to blow out **naturally**, but with a little added support from the **stomach muscles.**

A very relaxing way to teach breathing is to ask your students to yawn without raising their shoulders. Yawning is the body's way of quickly sending oxygen to the blood supply. You will notice yourself in trying this how quickly and fully air moves into the lungs. **The important lesson is to draw the breath in quickly and let the stomach expand out so that the lungs fill completely**.

Once the student learns proper breathing you can begin to instruct proper **blowing**. Eventually students begin to figure this all out intuitively, but I have a fun technique that starts them thinking about **controlled breath support** early. Light a candle and place it on a table about 18 inches away. Ask them to blow it out. That's easy! Now relight it and ask them to just make the flame flicker **without** blowing it out. That's a little harder. Now ask them to make it flicker **steadily** until they run out of breath. If you try this technique yourself you will find that in order to make the candle flicker and not go out, the breath must be very controlled. You will quite **naturally** use your stomach muscles to accomplish this. After the demonstration ask them if they felt anything in their stomach area. They will probably tell you they noticed a tightening there. These are exactly the muscles they must focus on when **blowing out** for good breath support.

Finally, an area that has been largely ignored is the manner in which students **physically support** the clarinet with their bodies. It is extremely important that the mouthpiece be held firmly in place and move as little as possible. Holding a clarinet is in and of itself a very unnatural task. The complication of fingering notes with the right hand while trying to hold the clarinet in position makes for a very clumsy and often frustrating experience. I wish all young students of the clarinet would be given neck straps from the very beginning. A neck strap will help in two very positive ways. First the weight is taken off the right hand so that there is no conflict between **supporting** the clarinet and **fingering**. Second, the neck strap can be adjusted so that the mouthpiece is consistently positioned in the mouth. This very simple and relatively inexpensive solution will make clarinet playing less frustrating for the young student and encourage better tone production and intonation.

Once students begin to progress into a level of fluency on the clarinet I think it is important to have them play in situations where they have a good pitch reference. For most of us this was playing duets with our teachers. As soon as possible have your students play solos with piano and as they become more adept have them play quartets among themselves. Young students are sponges and **will** begin to use their ears very soon if it is expected of them.

The suggestions offered here have been very basic. As students develop, the improvement of intonation becomes a matter of refinement of technical skills and ear training. I cannot stress enough the importance of using a **good tuning device** as an adjunct to good musical training. Consistent use of a tuner will help students assess problems in their playing and or equipment. For young students, an excellent first use of a tuner to check pitch generation is very simple. Have the student play with **mouthpiece and barrel only**. With a good **mouth-piece**, a firm **embouchure** and proper **breath support**, they should be able to generate a relatively in-tune **concert F-sharp.** ➔●

Musical Modeling: A Method for Developing Musical Expression

Edward Fraedrich

Teaching students to go beyond the markings on the page is one of the most critical challenges teachers face. How do we develop a student's innate musical ability without imposing our own musical ideas on him or her? How do students learn the difference between reproducing the symbols on the page and interpreting the music that the composer has written? Here are two versions of a recipe for helping students develop musical expression that I hope will inspire you to come up with your own variations.

INGREDIENTS:
Recordings of great performances of great music, the corresponding sheet music for those pieces, colored pencils, sensitive ears, an expressive heart, and a zeal to say more with the music that one plays

SERVES:
Anyone who wants to be a more expressive performer.

1. Comparative Listening

Give the student at least two recordings of the same piece—it may be a short, romantic piece for solo instrument, an art song, or a larger work such as a concerto—by artists who have different, but highly respected, interpretations of that work. I have used Chopin *Preludes*, Schumann songs, and the Tchaikovsky *Violin Concerto*, and all have worked well for this exercise. It works best if the music is written for an instrument other than that which the student plays—this will keep him from focusing on the technical aspects of the performance and will allow him to concentrate on the musicality of the performance.

For example, give the student recordings of the Tchaikovsky *Violin Concerto* with the following violinists: Jascha Heifitz, David Oistrakh, Itzhak Perlman, and Gil Shaham. These performances are very different from each other, and each performer interprets the music in ways not written in the published version of the music. Have the student listen carefully to the exposition of one version of the piece and note on the score, in pencil, how the performance differs from what is written on the page. The differences may be in tempo, dynamics, articulation, tone color, etc. Have the student write a short description of what those changes bring to the piece and what he or she likes or dislikes about those changes. Then, with a different recording, repeat the process using a different colored pencil. Continue with a different color for each recording.

Next compare the interpretations of the piece. Find changes that are shared by all the performers and changes that are unique to one performer. Impress on the student that these differences are not mistakes, but deliberate artistic choices made by the performer with the intention of improving the expressive qualities of the piece. Discuss just how different the interpretations of the music are and point out that each is equally valid.

Finally, ask the student to come up with a hybrid interpretation, combining elements of all the performances into a version that the student prefers to any one performer's version—he may also include changes that he prefers that are not found in any of the performances. By making this choice, the student has not only begun to make artistic decisions on his own, but is beginning to develop an independent musical style. Encourage the student to repeat this process with more music from different genres.

Note: Live recordings are often more musically spontaneous and offer students the additional insight that great performances are not ruined by the presence of a few missed notes.

2. Classical Transcription
Give the student a recording of a short art song and have him learn to play the piece without having seen the music. The student should copy the performance from the recording as closely as possible, matching the rubato, dynamics, tone changes, and every inflection of the performer. Encourage the student to play along with the recording and listen to it until he or she knows every nuance the performer makes on the recording. Have the student notate what is played, including each dynamic change, articulation, tempo change, etc. Then, show the student the music and let him see just how much that he has strayed from the printed music. The song cycles of composers such as Schumann and Schubert are excellent choices for this project. There are many outstanding recordings of these songs that offer a wealth of interpretations for the student to study.

Musicians in nonclassical fields like jazz and pop music have been doing this for years, and many musicians in those fields are virtually self-taught, their primary instruction on their instrument coming from what they transcribed from recordings.

Using this approach, the student will not only learn intimately the musical ideas of a great singer such as Renée Fleming or Dietrich Fischer-Dieskau, but will also realize just how much thought and attention to detail it takes to perform a seemingly simple song, and by extrapolation, the enormous task of thoroughly interpreting a concerto or large sonata.

Needless to say, it would be a good idea for the teacher to do this project before assigning it to the student. Not only will you benefit from the exercise, but you will be better able to discuss the process with the student. ➙

Instant First Sounds on the Flute—An Appetizer for Fun and Success

Laurie Glencross

In many conversations over the years with public school band directors, I have heard a common and recurring stew of complaints about their students' frustrating first attempts to make a sound on the flute. Why did that eager student who was so full of potential, enthusiasm, and excitement to learn, become a deflated soufflé, fallen flat? Can we avoid watching an intelligent youngster hit The Wall right away, giving up the flute in favor of an "easier" path to music making on another instrument or, worst of all, giving up musical aspirations altogether?

Band teachers and beginning flute teachers alike can be at a loss to find a recipe that really works at this crucial early learning phase. How can this process be more successful for both student and teacher? How can we shape success in easy bites that almost any student can digest? Can we whip up a foolproof concoction?

Satisfaction comes from making a sound. It's that simple. Now, here's how to make that happen!

INGREDIENTS:
One quart-sized plastic storage bag (no holes) or a party balloon
One drinking straw
One flute head-joint
A dash of creativity
A pinch of fun

SERVES:
Any and all frustrated future flutists and their facilitators.

PREPARATION:
Beginning wind players in general have little or no concept of the connection between breathing and sound production. Here are some ways to demonstrate this connection:

While standing, raise your arms in front of you, bend your elbows and point your forearms toward each other. Put the knuckles of your fists together and point your fingers toward your stomach just above your belt. Release all your air, right down to the bottom. Press your fingers into your stomach to push out the last little bits of air. Now, breathe in deeply through your nose *and* mouth and push your fingers away from you using your expanding stomach (diaphragm). Do this several times to get the feeling of the kind of low, full breath that you'll need to play the flute.

Now, holding a full breath, place the palm of your hand against your closed mouth. Blow against your hand but hold the air in. Feel the pressure of your breath against your hand. Now, take your hand away suddenly and feel the quick release of air. This is the kind of air volume you will need to play the flute. (Not for sissies!)

Take the plastic bag or balloon. Make a circle with your thumb and index finger just below the open end of the bag and create a small opening in the gathered plastic—just like a balloon. Take a BIG breath and blow into the bag or balloon to inflate it. This is the kind of sustained air pressure you will need to play the flute. (Are you dizzy yet? Don't cheat and start with a bag that already has air in it.)

Take a straw and hold it between your lips with your lips loose and forward as if you were saying, "Pooh." (No tight, "smiley" lips, please!) Place the straw into the opening of the bag and inflate the bag this way. (Easier? Your air stream is more concentrated with the straw and fills the bag faster and easier.)

Cooking with Gas
Now, let's kick it up a notch and apply these ideas to the flute head-joint. (For beginner flutists it is unnecessary to play the fully assembled instrument during the first lesson or even during the first week. The head-joint is the major sound producer and it is best to have some control over this part first before proceeding on to attempt to play the entire instrument.)

Take your head-joint from the flute case and leave the other parts in there—we won't need them for a while. Turn the head-joint so that the stopped end is on your left and the open end is on your right. Place the embouchure hole on top and angled toward you so that you can look into the hole. Hold it with your left hand grasping under the stopped end. (Don't be afraid to experiment with the head-joint for a few minutes. Look it over and blow into it in various ways and see what happens. Can you make a sound? Probably not, because the flute is so different than any other instrument.)

Take the straw you were using and hold it between your lips in the same manner you were doing previously—shape your lips loosely and forward as if you were saying, "Pooh." Holding the end of the straw with your right hand, direct this end at the embouchure hole of the head-joint and blow through it. Again, experiment and see if its possible to make a sound—probably not if you direct the straw straight down the hole, but try angling it across the hole so that the air hits the far wall of the embouchure hole. The flute is called an "edge-blown" instrument because of this property of making sound by splitting the air column you blow against the far edge of the hole. Some of your air should go into the flute while some of it is blown right across the opening.

Continue blowing (taking little breaks so you don't faint) until you can get a consistent sound though the straw the first time you try. The quality of the sound at this point doesn't matter, but make sure you are using a healthy and sustained stream of air.

Final Stir of the Pot
Put the straw down. Shape your lips just as you have been doing all along—"Pooh," no smiles— and bring the flute head-joint up to your lips. Place the embouchure plate/hole just below the rim of your lower lip. Lick your lips so they are moist. Imagine the straw's small opening and part your lips only that much in order to concentrate the air column. Blow a sustained stream of air, directing it toward that opposite wall of the opening just as you did with the straw. With some luck (and some practice), *you should now be getting a sound!* (Yippee, yahoo,

fireworks!) If not, go back to the straw for a while and try again later. There's no train to catch, hopefully, so you can take your time at this.

Icing on the Cake
Here are some more activities you can do with the flute head-joint that will make practicing all you've learned more fun.

Use your palm to cover the open end of the head-joint and blow. This should sound different than when the end was open. The sound can be lower if you blow softly or higher if you blow harder. Alternate blowing with the end stopped or open and see how the sound changes.

Gradually slide your finger over the open end of the head-joint while you blow to make a slide-whistle effect.

Slide you finger into the open end of the head-joint to make an even *better* slide-whistle. Careful—don't get your finger stuck! (This has happened.)

Play the song, "Merrily We Roll Along" by inserting the tip of your finger into the tube to find the three different pitches you need for this song.

Experiment and explore! Have some fun! Find some new sounds on your new instrument. ➤●

(Acknowledgment: The original drinking straw idea is attributed to Patricia George's "Flute Spa," presented at Millikin University in November 2002.)

A Recipe for Jazz Improvisation

Victor L. Goines

As with any dish that someone is hoping to prepare for a nice dinner or event, the most difficult thing is getting started. Jazz improvisation is no exception to this process. But once we start in motion, each individual has the ability to develop his or her very unique delicacy.

INGREDIENTS:
Recording device
Jazz recordings (Miles Davis–*Kind of Blue*; Louis Armstrong–*Hot Fives and Sevens*; Billie Holiday–*The Silver Collection*; Ella Fitzgerald–*Live in Berlin*; Sarah Vaughan–*Crazy and Mixed Up*; and many others.)
The voice (and personal instrument for non-vocalist)
Manuscript paper
Jamie Abersold–*Nothin' but the Blues* and Miles Davis *Kind of Blue* (play-along)

SERVES:
All musicians (students and instructors).

Getting started in jazz improvisation can be very intimidating for the average musician, but it doesn't have to be. The first thing that should be realized is that to improvise is a very natural event. In actuality, all of us improvise daily. Improvisation is a part of what we do as people. And jazz, while it seems foreign to most, doesn't have to be that way. Just think of it as a language–a foreign language, but a language. And the more you work on the vocabulary of the language, the more familiar you will become with the language of jazz, thus allowing you to participate in the language of jazz improvisation.

The first ingredient we need to create our dish is "courage." Actually, "The Courage to Create." This is probably the most important ingredient. In order for any musician to have any amount of success, he or she has to have the courage to take a chance. And in taking a chance, it is important not to qualify whether or not it is good or bad, but access or critique for what worked and what needs to be refined.

Secondly we will start by using the first musical instrument known to man–the voice. The reason for singing is that this removes the obstacle of identifying fingerings on the instrument. Quite often the idea of knowing which pitch goes with what sound can create an unnecessary challenge for anyone at first. But the voice allows us to sing whatever we hear in our inner ear. Think about, when we are walking up the street whistling or singing, we don't try to figure out the fingerings for the music we are creating. We just do it! Haven't you heard that before? But it is true.

For most of us, the idea of just singing whatever we are hearing sounds very abstract. This is where the ingredient "jazz recordings" comes in. It is important that everyone listens to historical recordings of jazz greats. This supplies a foundation for our vocabulary. For example, if someone wanted to be a writer, he or she couldn't just starting writing without any background or vocabulary. The same is true in jazz improvisation. We have to listen to experts in jazz music and extract vocabulary from their solos that will become a starting point for us to work with. This is called *transcribing*. *Transcribing* is the process of listening to a recorded performance and learning the performance by singing it and/or playing it on your specific instrument. Sometimes musicians write out these transcriptions for archival purposes. I personally write my transcriptions out because it supports my overall musicianship. Transcribing and listening are very important processes.

Now that you have transcribed a solo, try singing it along with the Jamie Abersold play-along series. This will allow you to work with a rhythm section. It would be ideal to perform with a live rhythm section but this is not always practical. Once you have tried singing the solo you transcribed, trying making up your own. Remember, it doesn't have to be all new material. You can take bits and pieces from the music you transcribed.

A bit of information for you: a very important device used in all jazz solos is *space*. Not the space that NASA travels to, but space in music known as *rest*. Quite often, musicians are so overwhelmed with what to play that they forget that it is probably better to play nothing—or rest. Try it out!

For our non-vocalist, it is time to transfer what we have been singing to our instruments. It is just a matter of becoming familiar with your instrument. In fact, I recommend that you think of your instrument as being an extension of your voice. In working on this process, you can practice by singing a note, then identifying it on your instrument. Or have a friend play a note on their instrument and you try to find the note on your instrument. The key to success in working on ear training is to go with your first instinct. You are trying to make it an instantaneous process. Jazz is a music that is in motion and requires that you be quick on your feet. Through practice, you will get better with time. *Don't get discouraged* if it takes longer for you than it does for a friend. Remember, everyone is an individual and has to deal with things in his or her own time frame.

So, you have been working primarily alone on your dish but the key to giving it more flavor is to get into a setting that allows you to interact with other musicians. Call up your friends and have a jam session. Record your session. Check out how you did. Check out what your friends did. Compare notes. Take some of your friends' ideas and interpret them into your own. If fact, place your individuality on their ideas. "*Spice 'em up*" so they won't even recognize them. Individuality is a very important part of jazz improvisation.

Our final ingredient, and maybe our most important one, is *perseverance*. Nothing will replace a great work ethic. If learning to improvise is a craft that you desire, you have to stick with it. As the saying goes, "*You will get out of it what you put into it.*" If you want to have a long conversation in jazz, you have to stick with it. Or as a football coach once told me, "*Winners never quit and quitters never win. Which one are you?*" I know that you are all winners, so never quit. Keep working on your craft and become the best improviser YOU can be. ➤●

Pulse and Tonic versus Beat and Key

Susan Goodfellow

All musicians want to play with accuracy, expression, and confidence. We practice ourselves into the ground trying to balance virtuosity and emotion and never losing control. And we tell our students to count and watch the key signature. I would like to suggest that these last two directives, while valid to a point, are limited in their ultimate value for achieving the harmonic and rhythmic control over a piece of music that ensures accuracy in performance.

INGREDIENTS:
Ears, an open mind, and security with scales and arpeggios

SERVES:
All instrumental musicians.

In a letter to the violinist Samuel Dushkin, Igor Stravinsky wrote, "Music is compared to mathematics. But in mathematics, there are infinite ways to arrive at the number 7. But with rhythm, the fact that they add up to 7 is of secondary importance. The important thing is, is it *5 and 2* or *2 and 5*? Because *5 and 2* is a different person from *2 and 5*."

It is axiomatic that every language has rhythmic cadence, and that we respond to that cadence. Similarly, music has cadence that goes beyond the numbers of counting. Numbers are static, whereas words are dynamic. Too seldom are students concerned with playing into a rhythmic cadence; if it can be understood as an extension of language, it is more likely to be both accurate and musical. For example, the Dutilleux "Sonatine" for flute and piano has a very difficult opening entrance for the flute. The time signature is 7/8 and the flute enters on a strong number in the counting system, which nevertheless has a weak pulse due to the syncopations in the piano part. But a sentence that fits the swing of the notes and rhythms of the phrase will make the entrance impossible to miss. Mine is: "White el-e-phants and small grey ones,/Large pa-chy-derms are NOW on dis-play." The flute enters at NOW, which gives both rhythmic and cognitive impetus to enter, and no one has missed it in years. Similar is the middle section of the third movement of the Martinu flute sonata, which is easy until played with the piano. The meter is 3/4, 5/4, 2/4, 5/4, 2/4, and the syncopations in the accompaniment can throw the best student off the track; however, I found that if one thinks the following: "See the hip-po-po-ta-mus eat/Ap-ples car-rots and peas/" with the long notes (2 beats apiece) on See, eat, peas, there is no confusion.

The point of this is that musical cadence is controlled by down- and up-pulses, like poetic feet, rather than beats. Many times transfer students come to me with their music marked with lines indicating half-beat subdivisions. That is tantamount to slicing cheese; it gives no room for up pulses and the music therefore has no swing; it is robotic, rather than poetic, language.

Words can also facilitate rhythmic modulation, whether a simple duple/triple alternation (as in the eighth note/triplet opening of the Chaminade "Concertino") or the more complex 10-note/14-note/16-note acceleration in the Lowell Liebermann "Soliloquy" for solo flute. It has been claimed that the brain internalizes entities up through 4 with a simple nerve firing between synapses; after that, the firing is complex. Therefore, it is logical to break groupings down into 4 or fewer no matter how fast or virtuosic the passage may be. Words lend themselves to these patterns by the aforesaid up and down pulses. If we think "Rab-bit, Por-cu-pine, Al-li-ga-tor, Hip-po-po-ta-mus, Pa-ra-le-gal-i-ty, Pa-chy-ce-pha-lo-saur-us," the swing of the words falls into groups of 4 or fewer, while internalizing a count of up to 7. An interesting example is the second of the "Three American Pieces" of Lucas Foss, which alternates 5-note measures pulsed between 2/3 and 3/2 at a very fast tempo with the piano not helping in the least. Safest is to think words: Hip-po-pot-a-mus versus ol-e-o-phil-ic works very well, especially when written above the notes in the part.

Then there is the question of key. We practice scales and all arpeggiated patterns in every key so that our ears seem to exist in our fingers: we hear a key and the hands go there. If we put that to work for us, we will pay attention to the immediate tonic of the passage, or even of the run or configuration, that we are playing. For example, the "Romance and Scherzo" for flute and piano by Gabriel Grovlez has three poisonous-looking runs in the opening movement: but if you understand that after the first note of each they are in D-flat, B-flat melodic minor, and C melodic minor, albeit not beginning on the tonic, there is no problem. Again from the Liebermann "Soliloquy," the fast descending and then ascending triplets, rife with accidentals, is formidable especially under performance pressure. However, if above those scary triplets the tonalities for each are indicated, they are playable with ease: B, F, A-flat, B-flat, F-sharp minor, D, F, A-flat, B, D, F.

Pianist Maurice Hinson has said that, "Every instrumental problem has both its origin and its solution in the music itself." I believe this to be true of many things that plague our performances. Try these suggestions as you study your music, and you may well find that it bakes up very well indeed. ➡•

My Director Taught Me the Wrong Fingerings!

Bruce Hammel

INGREDIENTS:
Students or teachers should be able to play at least a one-octave F major scale on the bassoon, for the full flavor of this recipe to be appreciated.

SERVES:
Any director or student who wants to play or teach bassoon . . . and get it right.

In the midst of writing this article, a new student arrived for his first bassoon lesson. He had been playing bassoon in band, however, and as is often the case, had learned many incorrect fingerings for some of the most basic notes. The day after our lesson he approached his band director (who is, incidentally, exceptionally good) and proclaimed, "You taught me the wrong fingerings!" Despite improved resources for the beginning bassoon student, effective communication of correct fingerings is an ongoing issue.

Almost every band or bassoon method book offers a fingering chart for the beginning bassoonist, and these charts have improved significantly over the years. Unfortunately, despite our best attempts to make fingerings clear and accurate, students often have difficulty interpreting the charts correctly. Some charts refer to specific keys using numbers or letters, and the student is unable to identify the correct keys. Other times, alternate fingerings are displayed alongside regular ones, and students adopt the alternate as their preferred fingering. The net result is a student battling to produce correct pitches, let alone good intonation, with "close, but no cigar" finger combinations.

My personal attempt to ameliorate this situation is to provide a clear and accurate fingering chart online (www.vcubassoon.org), complete with close-up photos of the keywork, annotations for each fingering, and a printable version to have with the student's music. This is no guarantee, however, that this resource will be utilized effectively by students without supervision. It is therefore incumbent upon ensemble directors to monitor their bassoon students' fingering habits. In the following paragraphs, I list the most common fingering errors, the characteristic sound they produce, and tips for remedying each problem.

Step 1 is to identify all of the keys and their functions. Below are images of a typical, good student instrument (Fox Renard) with all keys labeled, with the exception of the tone holes. Most student bassoons do not include the high D and high E keys as pictured here—don't despair, they are not of much use to any but the most advanced players. Once you have familiarized yourself with the keys, proceed to learn about the most common problems students have in using them properly.

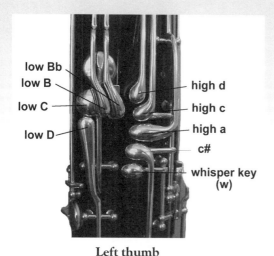

Left thumb

Left hand

Right thumb

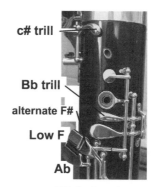

Right hand

The lowest notes on the bassoon (B-flat^2-F^2) can generally only be produced if the correct fingering is used. If a student is unable to produce these tones, then there is a strong possibility that a finger or two has been misplaced (provided the

instrument is in good working order). The most common problems in this register are generally not with incorrect fingerings, but with fingers that slip off of the open holes, even if ever so slightly. The primary culprits are the left hand ring and middle fingers.

In the next octave, G-flat/F-sharp#^{2} has two acceptable fingerings, right thumb or right pinky. Most beginners have a difficult time reaching the "alternate" G-flat/F-sharp key with their pinky, so the thumb one is usually the one they adopt.

Fortunately, this is the preferred fingering—the alternate is used primarily to free the thumb up for playing B-flat in passages requiring this. The tuning of the two fingerings is usually somewhat different; the alternate fingering is often somewhat flatter in pitch. This is helpful for the upper octave (G-flat/F-sharp^3) where the pitch is usually quite sharp.

The A-flat/G-sharp^2 (and the octave higher) also has a regular and an alternate, but rarely do students prefer the alternate (in part, because many student bassoons don't have the required key!).

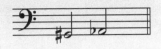

On most bassoons, there is a special trill key for B-flat^2 (and the octave higher) which lies between the 3rd and 4th fingers of the right hand. Many students believe this is a rather con-

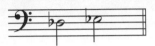

venient location for the B-flat key despite the problem it causes when trying to move the 4th finger to the G key.

Moving higher still, B, C, D, E, and F in this register are rarely, if ever, misunderstood, but many students neglect to use the whisper key unless reminded. The remaining two notes, C-sharp/D-flat^2 and D-sharp/E-flat^2, however, can be confusing. The C-sharp/D-flat requires the left thumb to hold down three keys simultaneously, the C-sharp key, whisper key, and low D key. This sounds more difficult than it is, but still creates some awkward motion for the thumb when changing notes. The D-sharp/E-flat is usually introduced as a simple "forked" fingering (left hand 1 and 3 fingers), but it is not much more difficult for students to use the full, more reliable fingering, which includes the B-flat key and middle finger with the right hand. With some reeds/instruments the difference may be subtle, but on others, profound.

Now the real fun begins! The three notes immediately above open F have two things in common—the whisper key should be down and the left hand index finger should slide down to open half of the tone hole (referred to as half-hole technique).

Failure to use the whisper key may not cause noticeable problems, but inadequate half-holing will produce a very ugly attack. Unfortunately, this is the method of choice for most young students. You may need to remind them frequently to half-hole in this range. An additional complicating factor with these three notes is that one of them, G, benefits significantly by using the left pinky E-flat key to lower the pitch and increase resonance. It generally detracts from the tone quality of its neighbors, and students often have difficulty incorporating this into their fingering repertoire. Keep reminding them—it will really improve that note.

The acoustic idiosyncrasies of the bassoon make the next group of notes devilishly hard to produce for many students. The crux of the problem is that the opening of the "octave key" (whisper key) is positioned too high up the

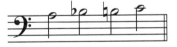

bore to be effective for these notes. Standard fingering charts simply provide the lower octave fingering absent the whisper key and in many cases this works fine. For students who have difficulty producing these notes consistently (and there may be many), there is a simple solution that is used by many professional bassoonists. The high C key can serve as a substitute "octave key" and will guarantee good response on these notes. The downside is that the key is operated by the left thumb and adds yet another thing for students to remember. Until they become aware of how bad the attacks on those notes are without help, you will need to encourage them to add the thumb.

For the final group of notes, one simple caveat—add the left pinky E-flat key for increased resonance. Inattention to this detail will not

cause serious harm, but students should be encouraged to use the best possible fingering at all times. ➤•

Basic Recipe for Determining the Direction of a Musical Phrase

Diana Haskell

INGREDIENTS:
Good ears and a musical heart

SERVES:
Other people with good ears and musical hearts.

What we say to one another is often filled with emotion of some sort. How a sentence is spoken determines character or mood. We share emotion with listeners through direction and inflection in our voice. Speak the following sentence out loud with marked indications:

✔ "Play from the soul, not like a trained bird." (C.P.E. Bach)

ff sempre_____ accel._____

✔ "Play from the soul, not like a trained bird."

p ⊏——————— mp, p ⊏——————— mp

✔ "Play from the soul, not like a trained bird."

pp_____ritard.____

Human speech is similar to musical phrasing in that both seek to share something with the listener. In the examples above, each version has different direction and thus, creates a distinctive mood. The first version is forceful and rushed, producing a feeling of fury or impatience. The second rendition is less hurried but with emphasis, creating a mood of quiet authority. The last is slower still and very soft, giving the sense of contained irritation or perhaps gentleness. Exploring direction of musical phrases can be done in much the same way as in speech.

Our music-making must be filled with direction and inflection . . . sometimes overt, sometimes imperceptible, often in between the two extremes. Nevertheless, direction must take place or music becomes stagnant and lifeless. How many times have we heard a performance where a work is played mistake-free, yet leaves our hearts cold?

We spend a great deal of time addressing technical issues: learning notes, perfecting embouchures, playing scales evenly, focusing on tonguing, tone, reeds, and ensemble playing. It's fun and necessary to work on technique. But what good are facile fingers and a great sound if there is little thought about musicianship? Technical ability (and performers) must always be in submission to the music.

A primary objective of music is to communicate a composer's musical thoughts to an audience. Musicians must learn to express musical gestures as a way to convey what we think a composer is saying, both individually and in a group.

One important way to express musical ideas is by giving *direction in phrasing*. Phrase direction maps the musical path through a piece. It is like a beacon of light that guides a listener into a greater understanding of music.

Below are some beginning ideas for phrase direction. I have in no way been exhaustive in this approach. Experiment with these concepts to go beyond the chains of technical drudgery. Phrase direction can be practiced individually or in ensemble playing, or during warm-ups or scales.

At first this approach may seem artificial or mannered but with time these ingredients will merge into a wonderful, natural feast where a pinch of this or a shake of that may be added. The more we practice the art of musicianship the freer we become as musicians.

I. Musical Staples: Flour and Sugar for Your Musical Pantry

A. Kitchen Rules

- There are usually several musical options for any given phrase. Be creative!
- Think of musical practice as experimentation. Sing the phrases or record them in different ways.
- Musical rules are made to be broken. (Example: In a passage marked *piano* there might be room for a crescendo to *mezzo forte* or *forte*, even if it's not shown in the music.)

B. Kitchen Tools

- A recording device
- Voice
- Instrument (s) and piece of music

II. Envisioning the Whole Meal: The Peak and Arch

Before experimenting with individual phrasing, it will be beneficial to find the peak and arch of the piece. Many times this culmination point is about 2/3 of the way through a piece, but that is not always the case. Look for one or more of the following:

1. The series of notes marked with the most forceful dynamics.
2. The highest series of notes.
3. The fastest sequence of notes.

After this peak is discovered, work all phrases from the beginning of the piece to the end with the idea that they all lead to or come away from that passionate moment. In other words, create a sense of anticipation that leads naturally to the peak, and then leads from it. This is the arch of the piece. Often finding the peak of a movement or work, especially something complex, will include analysis of the harmonic structure.

III. Hunting for Game or Where are the Phrases?

A phrase can be a measure or less, several measures long, made up of two or more subphrases or be rather extended. Most often there are several ways to phrase a passage. Be open to altering initial impressions. It might be helpful at first to lightly bracket phrases and modify them as confidence is gained.

As a simple example, "Row Your Boat" can be either divided into four phrases, two phrases, or one long phrase.

Four-phrase: *Row, row, row your boat/gently down the stream;/merrily, merrily, merrily, merrily,/ life is but a dream.*

Two-phrase: *Row, row, row your boat, gently down the stream;/merrily, merrily, merrily, merrily, life is but a dream.*

One-phrase: *Row, row, row your boat, gently down the stream; merrily, merrily, merrily, merrily, life is but a dream.*

The reader may ask: which option is the "best?" While all are fine, many musicians will opt for longer phrase lines. Musicians often change phrasing from performance to performance. However, variations are usually thought out ahead of time in the practice room or rehearsal hall.

IV. Main Course: Smaller Peaks

In almost every phrase, just as in an overall work, there is a peak and an arch. While the guidelines for finding the peak of a phrase are similar, here are some additional suggestions. Look for the:

- highest note(s) of the phrase
- lowest note(s) of the phrase
- longest note(s) of the phrase
- the loudest or softest note(s)

Now we are ready to give the phrase some direction.

V. Musical Chefs

Once the peak of a phrase is discerned, use approaches below to create an arch of sound. There are many ways to show the arch of a phrase, including:

- Air stream or bow speed
- Volume
- Vibrato: add, change speed of, or eliminate
- Articulation: change lengths and qualities
- Tone: clear, bright, covered, open
- Timing: rubato, ritardando, tenuto, accelerando

There are endless choices. If calmness is desired, perhaps less vibrato, softer volume, and gentler articulations will be employed. If a change of key is involved, color change can show modulation well. This subject is difficult to quantify. Much time, study, and listening must take place to come up with convincing phrase direction. Unlike computers, there is no instant fix. However, there is no greater joy than sharing a part of oneself with an audience through music. ➤●

Successful Intonation Is More Than a Matter of Good Taste!

Wayne Hedrick

This is a recipe for successful intonation and is a guide for players who may be struggling with tuning. The recipe is written by a flutist, but it is intended for any musician.

INGREDIENTS:
The most common mistake is to leave out an ingredient. Our ingredients are:
A good instrument
Some basic knowledge about intonation fundamentals
Know that your instrument is intentionally "out of tune"
The skill of playing both sharp and flat
A decent warm-up
A thick skin

SERVING SUGGESTIONS:
Play the role you are assigned
"The Secret's in the Sauce"

SERVES:
This recipe will serve one woodwind musician at a time for the duration of a career.

A Good Instrument
A significant ingredient is the quality of your instrument, and the most important component of your instrument is its scale. Woodwind players must also utilize the services of a great repair technician to keep their instruments in perfect condition. Tiny changes to woodwind key heights can make amazing changes to an instrument's pitch.

However, you, the player, are the responsible party and you may not blame your instrument if a note is out of tune. Good intonation happens when a competent player controls the sounds of his or her instrument and matches those sounds to the rest of the ensemble. I have frequently observed two consistent behaviors: 1) A great player will play a $300 flute in tune, but she will just have to work harder. 2) A poor player will play a $20,000 flute out of tune and think it sounds great, knowing the flute is expensive.

There are many recordings of the famous flutist William Kincaid. Through most of his career, Kincaid preferred a platinum Powell flute that he bought in 1939. Although Kincaid's platinum flute is priceless today, it was not manufactured with twenty-first-century technology and computer controlled lathes. Nonetheless, Kincaid's intonation was immaculate because he controlled the sounds that his instrument produced.

Some Basic Knowledge About Intonation Fundamentals

Music requires many different intonation systems. Enter "musical tuning," "just intonation," and "equal temperament" in www.google.com and www.wikipedia.com.

In general, ensembles use just intonation. In just intonation, the pitch adjusts to each tonal center. Properly tuned, pitches can vary over one-third of a step, as compared to the piano or a digital tuner. Just intervals are based on ratios that get complicated as the chords get farther away from the tonic. It is a mathematical impossibility that one could always be correct as the musical tonal center changes. Regardless, we are expected to sound perfect, and the only solution is to adjust so quickly that we avoid being obvious.

On the other hand, fixed-pitch instruments generally use equal temperament. Equal temperament works for fixed-pitch instruments because it sounds acceptable to our ears and allows these instruments to play in all the keys, all just a tiny bit out of tune.

Intonation gets interesting when an ensemble has to play with the piano (or xylophone, or bells, or organ). When that line is prominent, the musicians stop tuning among themselves and start matching the fixed-pitch instruments. The rules: When playing with ensembles, match the other players or you are out of tune. When playing a line with a fixed-pitched instrument, match it or you will be the villain. Adjust quickly!

Know That Your Instrument Is Intentionally "Out of Tune."

All woodwind instruments are intentionally built out of tune. The C-sharp in the staff on a $30,000 flute will still be sharp. The finest clarinet in the world has sharp throat tones. The top saxophone still has sharp palm keys. Our instruments have to be this way; it is not an engineering mistake. Woodwind intonation is a mechanical compromise because one hole can serve many roles.

For example, the clarinet's throat B-flat uses the register key. The position, shape, size, and vent height are a compromise between the pitch of the B-flat and register key function. The pitch of this B-flat can be lowered by moving the hole down the clarinet, but this will also negatively affect the register functions. A clarinet needs a great register key because it affects two-thirds of the clarinet's range. The clarinetist must always be aware of these compromises and help his clarinet play in tune, in spite of its limitations.

Another example is the flute's C-sharp in the staff, which is a compromise between the pitch of the C-sharp and venting for the second D and E-flat, the D above the staff and top A-flat, top A, and top B-flat. If the hole is lowered for the C-sharp in the staff, the venting of all of the other notes are negatively affected.

Almost all flutes have a standard C-sharp. We have to produce C-sharp on an instrument that has the hole in the wrong place for good reasons and have to play that note much flatter than the flute's natural sound. We cannot blame our instrument; it is our responsibility to compensate for these problems, just as Kincaid did.

The Skill of Playing Both Sharp and Flat

Develop the skills to learn to play a little high and a little low. In practice, you will rarely be able to play at your instrument's comfortable pitch. To begin with, woodwind instruments react differently to volume. Play loudly and the flutes go sharp while the clarinets go flat. You can compensate with your embouchure and air stream. In addition, you can adjust the head/mouthpiece/body joints as necessary to fit into the ensemble. Some players will adjust their head/mouthpiece/body for extended soft passages or extended loud passages. You can also use alternate fingerings to stay out of trouble. There are encyclopedias of fingering charts for woodwinds; see the author's example at www.larrykrantz.com/whedrick.htm. Be prepared to go sharp or flat at any time!

A Decent Warm-up

Wind instruments produce different pitches at different temperatures. A 50-degree wood-wind will not produce the same pitches as it does when the metal/wood is at 72 degrees. More importantly, instruments respond to temperature changes at different rates. So, you should always arrive early. Warm the instrument and yourself up in the performance room and then worry about intonation. You are ready to tune when everything is stabilized (up or down) to the room's temperature.

A Thick Skin

Musicians must have a thick skin; they have to be able to accept criticism. When a conductor or an oboe player says, "You're sharp," treat it as observation of the noise you produced, and not as a personal attack. Simply play at a lower pitch and move on.

SERVING SUGGESTIONS:

Now that we have the basic ingredients, it is time to serve this recipe in a performance.

Play the Role You Are Assigned

The wind section has well-defined roles. The principal players are responsible for the pitch level of the section and intonation between the sections. When the flutes are sharp to the clarinets, the principal flute and principal clarinet are responsible. One of them must yield to resolve this conflict or the passage remains out of tune.

The second and third chair players have entirely different roles. Their first job is to match their principal player. If the flutes are out of tune, it is a failure of the second or third flute players. If the clarinets are out of tune, the section clarinets are to blame. Additionally, there are also innumerable examples where the second flute, oboe, and clarinet make up a new "section." These musicians also have to yield to each other.

The rules change as musical situations evolve continuously in the score. As a musician, you have to lead for one phrase, follow for the next phrase, and always be aware of your role within the fabric of the music at the instant that you are playing.

"The Secret's in the Sauce"

The great chefs of the world prepare fantastic sauces to make their food special. The sauces must complement the main ingredients to bring the flavors to life. No one enjoys BBQ sauce on cupcakes. No one serves hot fudge on prime rib.

In our recipe, a musician's "sauce" is the player's attitude, which must complement the musical situation. An attitude of "I'm right and you're wrong" or "My intonation is correct" will ruin your relationships with your fellow musicians. "Right" and "wrong" are often combative words in intonation. Even if you are absolutely correct, such an attitude is the unpleasant equivalent of that BBQ sauce on cupcakes.

The proper attitude is to think of "matching," "helping," and "yielding." As a team player in a woodwind section, make the other players sound their best by matching what they produce.

Help match the clarinet in the throat tones and yield to the immovable oboe. It will not be news to the clarinetist if you tell her that her throat tones are sharp, but she will think you are wonderful if you match her as she tries to bring them in line.

The title of the recipe begins with "Successful Intonation . . . " not "Perfect Intonation . . . ." Our objective should not be to play "perfectly in tune," because such a goal is unattainable. The great flutist Peter Lloyd says that it is more practical to attempt to play "perfectly out of tune with the other players." The trick to playing "perfectly out of tune with your friends" is simply to yield and get past the intonation problems successfully.

Adapt to the musical environment and play your position. Lead when you have the responsibility, and yield to the other players as necessary. When playing second flute, track the first flute but pay particular attention to the second oboe and the second clarinet.

Always serve the recipe with a full "can" of sauce. When the clarinet is sharp, you "can" play sharp to make the two instruments sound as one. The oboe is flat; you "can" be flat to make the two instruments sound pleasant. With a good attitude towards yielding, some knowledge of your role, and some flexibility, successful intonation is achievable and your performances will be enjoyable to all concerned. ➙●

Build on What You Already Know—A Different Way to Approach Improvisation

Rob Holmes

Taking the first step toward attempting jazz improvisation can be a terrifying experience for both the novice and accomplished musician. Many performers feel insecure about creating music on the spot with no notes to read off of a page or seemingly no definitive instruction about what to play. Even musicians with the incredible gift of perfect pitch can doubt their own abilities as soon as music is removed from view and the daunting goal of spontaneous creation is presented as the only option. The unfortunate thing about our irrational fears toward this creative process is that it can be incredibly satisfying and invigorating to attempt. If music is a language all its own, then improvisation takes this beautiful language to a different level by allowing players to engage in intimate, spur-of-the-moment conversation. Here are some basic building blocks that will help to alleviate the anxiety of attempting to create new melodies and rhythms on the spot. Incorporating these building blocks will add a whole new dimension to any performer's abilities and can liberate one from feeling handcuffed to the written note. At the very least, they will provide a new approach to music study by demonstrating a willingness to think outside the box.

INGREDIENTS:
Attempting this recipe will require good facility and technique on an instrument, a basic understanding of major scales, and a good handle on interpreting rhythmic variation.

SERVES:
All instrumentalists.

Everyone who has studied music has been asked, or in some cases, forced to learn major scales. Scale studies absolutely provide the necessary foundation for good musicianship. Stable tone production, good technique, and endurance are all accomplished through scale studies. A student who has memorized major scales and common variations, including arpeggios and alternating intervallic studies such as thirds and fourths, will have a solid groundwork from which to work.

While I was studying music composition in graduate school, I had a professor who asked me a question that caused me to think about major scales in a whole new way. It occurred to me that the answer to this particular question could also be an interesting way to approach improvisation. The question was, "How many different major scales are there?" My first reaction was that I was in the wrong class—of course I already knew that there were twelve different major scales, which directly corresponded to the twelve key centers. Much to my chagrin, I was incorrect. "There is only one major scale," my professor stated matter-of-factly.

One major scale? How could this be? What did she mean . . . exactly? Since a major scale is made up of a certain combination of whole steps and half steps and all major scales share the same combination, then there is only one major scale. Her logic was correct. Of course twelve different starting points doesn't change the fact that the combination of notes doesn't change in a major scale. It is the twelve different starting notes that only give the impression of twelve different scales. Could it then be true that it was possible to know all of the major scales just from knowing one scale combination? The answer was yes.

The important lesson that I took from this exchange was to be willing to accept other viewpoints. Even something as seemingly monotonous as scales can provide a basis for new insight if you allow yourself to be open to other angles and options. This is the framework for beginning to build on what you already know regarding improvisation. A good improviser doesn't limit possibilities.

Take the C major scale as an example. Instead of only allowing yourself to practice the C major scale from root position to root position, extend the range. Use your knowledge of the key signature (no sharps or flats), and practice the scale from other starting points and stop in new places. You will discover that once you know the C major scale, you actually know seven different scales. If the idea of improvisation is to create new melodies, and scales are the basis for this creativity, then why limit yourself by only knowing the scale from its root position? Any one of the notes in a major scale can be a starting point. In fact, these starting points are called modes. Learning the modes of a major scale is a good idea, but playing them is something you can already do just from knowing your major scales. These particular scale studies will open your ears to new intervallic combinations and help to shape and personalize melodic ideas. Use the tools you already have to expand melodic and harmonic possibilities.

The next step is to combine rhythmic variation with this new approach to scale study. While practicing scales with a metronome and keeping a steady pace is valuable, practicing scales while varying your rhythmic pulse can be liberating. Pick a key center you are comfortable with and try to stay in that key for at least 5 minutes. Be sure to limit yourself to only notes within that key center. Every time you pause to take a breath, start on a new note within that key. Vary the octaves you start and stop in. Really try to get the sound of that key in your ear. Actively listen to what you are playing and try to internalize all of the melodies you come up with. Keep your rhythmic approach simple until you really have the sound of the key in your ear. By attempting these techniques, you will be opening your mind to the idea of free expression by using exercises that you already know. In a sense, you are tricking your mind into thinking that you are attempting something brand new when in fact you are merely teaching yourself to extend your rock-solid foundation into something more innovative.

Congratulations! You are already improvising. ➤●

The Seduction of the Ear: The Art of Creating a Beautiful Sound

Bil Jackson

INGREDIENTS:
The ability to really listen to your sound and the willingness to analyze and improve

SERVES:
Music lovers and performers.

The most important aspect of clarinet artistry is sound. It's what people hear first. If your sound is unpleasant, it doesn't matter if you can craft a phrase or demonstrate blazing technique, because few will listen. The final arbiter in all matters musical is the ear. This discussion will focus on three physical fundamental concepts essential in creating a beautiful sound: breathing, configuration of the oral cavity, and embouchure. There is another essential element, which is aesthetic in nature. This element is an accurate concept of your ideal sound. Additionally, you *must* have a good quality reed, mouthpiece, and instrument.

A Pinch of Breathing
Proper inhalation requires knowing how to fill your entire lung capacity efficiently. As you inhale, strive for full expansion in the lower back as well as in the abdomen. Place one hand on your sternum and the other on your abdomen, about belt level. Slowly and steadily draw in air, as if inhaling through a large straw. Focus on expanding your lungs completely in the area of your lower hand, then, allow the upper part of your lungs to fill. Observe your two hands to validate that the lower hand expands first. Exhaling is essentially the reverse of inhaling, with one important difference. Keeping your hands in the previously mentioned positions, exhale with the same slow and steady straw-like air stream, but don't let the lower hand collapse inward as you exhale. Push "down and out" with the abdomen while you exhale. The lower hand should collapse only at the very end of your exhalation.

A helpful visualization compares "hot" air "to "cold" air. "Hot" air is produced when you breathe condensation on your glasses to clean them. The "hahhh" sound is generated in the upper part of your lungs and is an unsupported way to exhale. Correct exhalation involves "cold air," which is generated in the lower abdomen. Visualize trying to blow out a candle four feet away, maintaining a steady and high-velocity air stream: visualize a laser-like beam of air directed at the candle.

Practice the "cold air" exercise with hands placed as previously mentioned. Don't let your abdomen collapse. Pushing "down and out" with the abdomen creates a more dense, supported air stream, the foundation of a beautiful sound. Remember, support is the dynamic combination of density/velocity of the air stream with density as the constant and velocity as the variable. Density creates "presence" or core of your sound and velocity controls dynamics.

A Dose of Oral Cavity

"O" with the mouth and "E" with the tongue is the secret. The oral cavity should be open, for resonance, and the tongue should be in a relatively high position to produce a fast air stream. To accomplish this, look in a mirror, and say "oh," as in the word "low." Strive for perfectly round lips and notice that your chin flattens naturally. Now, without moving your lips, say the vowel "E" and allow your tongue, but not your lips, to elevate in your mouth. The resulting phonic should sound like the syllable "Ich" in German. I know it's like patting your head and rubbing your tummy, but it's important to have the independence of the physical configurations. This configuration accomplishes two things. First, it speeds up the velocity of the air stream. The faster the velocity of air, the more the reed vibrates, resulting in more control. Second, it places the tongue in the optimum position for efficient articulation. Visualize directing, then reflecting, a dense, and to reiterate, laser-like supported air stream off the back of your incisors.

Another way to reference this formation is to finger the G-sharp right above the staff using the first two fingers of the left hand, and the first two fingers of the right (with of course the register key and thumb) This fingering is normally used for fast technical passages but is additionally a fantastic technique for intuiting the physical location and surface profile of the tongue.

A Dash of Embouchure

The last stop of the air stream is the embouchure. Here is how to form a naturally stable embouchure in three easy steps.

First, set the lower jaw/lower lip configuration. The jaw/lower lip configuration is the foundation of the embouchure. A helpful exercise is to imagine that your lower lip is divided into three equal parts. Try to squeeze the middle third with the outer two "thirds" while maintaining a flat chin. The sensation you create in your facial muscles is similar in feeling to a correct embouchure. Another option is to mimic a trumpet embouchure. Put your lips together and create a buzzing sound like a trumpet player. Strive to create a straw-sized area that buzzes and observe the physical sensations. If the muscles of your embouchure when you are playing the clarinet don't feel similarly, you will know where you need improvement. Important! Don't thrust your chin forward in either example. Keep it in a natural position. The amount of lower lip that naturally covers your lower teeth as a result of either exercise is the correct amount for your physical makeup.

Second, while maintaining either of the previous configurations, slide the mouthpiece into your mouth. After you set the profile outlined in the previous paragraph, slide the mouthpiece into your mouth. It's very important to note that once the profile is set, it does not move! If you move, start over. When the mouthpiece contacts the top teeth, stop. This stop point will be contingent on the angle at which you hold the clarinet and the profile of the "beak" of your mouthpiece. It's important to hold the instrument no more than 30-40 degrees from parallel to your face, assuming your orthodontic occlusion is normal.

Third, draw in the corners of the mouth and bring the upper lip down to the mouthpiece. Imagine drawing the strings of a coin purse together—but *only* with the corners and upper lip and not the jaw/lower lip!

It's important to understand that an embouchure is a controlled bite. Teachers often tell their students, "Don't bite." What they really mean is, "Don't bite excessively." It takes a degree of pressure on the reed to focus reed vibration optimally. We use the sides of the mouth and the upper lip to control excessive jaw pressure. Remember, the function of the embouchure is to provide the *optimum environment for the vibration of the reed.* ➡●

Shifting Our Values: Music Performance vs. Music Education

Celeste Johnson

INGREDIENTS:
The desire to teach music
Basic intelligence

SERVES:
Aspiring teachers and generations of students.

Upon deciding to become music majors, most students then face the decision of whether to veer towards a performance degree or music education. Many factors go into this important decision; some can easily see themselves teaching music in the public schools, others can't imagine conducting a band, orchestra, or choir. Some musicians may also know from an early age that they want a career in performing, commonly striving to perform in a professional orchestra or military band. Whichever direction a music student decides to go, it is of the utmost importance that throughout their collegiate training, they are held to a high standard of musicianship and dedication.

When a music major decides to pursue a performance degree, their teacher will most likely put them through a series of etudes, scales, practice techniques, excerpts, and solos. The general expectation is that the performance major will practice for numerous hours a day, learn a great deal of standard orchestral and solo repertoire, put on several recitals during their bachelor's degree, and possibly dedicate several summers to even more training and lessons at summer festivals—the goal being acceptance into a graduate program for even further training, or to be lucky enough to win a job through the process of an audition. It is generally known that this field is extremely competitive, with musicians frequently having to take dozens of auditions after years of stringent practicing in hopes of landing a gig.

When someone decides to become a music education major, they are promised a much more stable and predictable career in teaching than those who opt for a music performance degree. The job openings are more frequent, and the placement rate in positions is much higher for those in music education than in performance degree programs. In addition to the continuing performance on their instruments, music education majors are also required to add education requirements to their curriculum. They will also spend a semester student teaching, and usually are required to spend hours doing observations of current music educators. Along with this job stability comes a great deal of responsibility, not only as a teacher and leader of these musical groups, but to the future of music in children and young adults. Their musicianship must be nothing but stellar to create a productive and enjoyable music program. They must be good at organizing events, and willing to spend extra hours in rehearsals, competitions, marching band, and other regional and state music events.

Often music education majors in college are held to a lesser standard than performance majors, and sadly I have seen numerous cases of this. Unfortunately, the expectations and standard of many music education majors across the country are lower than what is expected of most performance majors. It seems that less is expected of them on their own instruments because their job prospects are so much more stable, and they will not necessarily be regularly performing on their instruments as a public school band, chorus, or orchestra conductor. Although these things are true, many aspects of good musicianship are learned through personal performance experience, a necessary prerequisite to teaching music. Often the important part of preparing for an important performance is not the actual performance, but the benefits seen from the process of practicing and learning the music. Although everyone will progress at various rates, all music majors are capable of musical growth and a level of dedication and practice techniques necessary to pursue a successful career in music.

My problem with this lower expectation of future music educators has many layers, and I strive to help my students who are music majors (regardless of area of specialty) be the best musicians and performers they are each capable of becoming. We as musicians learn to perform largely through experience. We learn to play musically, stylistically, and in tune through performing solos or in ensembles. In learning various etudes or music, we learn to not only perform, but also the process through which music is learned, rehearsed, and executed. These skills of learning, rehearsing, and executing good performances are essential to the successful music educator, and the higher level of experience and depth of knowledge they have in this area, the more successful they will be as an educator. The depth of knowledge in repertoire, and ability to communicate this process, is vital. They are also the representation of a professional musician to many students, and may be asked for advice or assistance from those students who take a particular interest in pursuing music at a higher level.

Music education majors are the future of the field of music. It is through these musicians that children and young adults are exposed to and participate in music. Although I realize this puts a great deal of responsibility on those who have chosen to pursue music education—to execute the same musical growth and dedication as someone who intends to become a performer—however with greater work also comes greater rewards. The more passionate the teacher is about music, the more this is conveyed to their students. It is my belief that music education majors are just as capable as those who choose to pursue a performing career, and I firmly believe that the stronger their background and training in music at the high school and collegiate level, the more successful they will become as a music educator, and the more enjoyment younger students will acquire through experiencing music themselves.

As a music educator myself, I constantly strive to continue performing at the highest level I am capable of. I hope that I can serve as an example of professionalism, but also provide some level of musical inspiration to my students. I value a high level of performing not only for my own satisfaction, but also because I teach, and choose to do what I expect of my own students. To continue striving to perform better, to practice well for performances, and continue learning and being passionate about the art of music, which we've all chosen to be a part of. A conductor once said to an orchestra I was playing in: "You're all here because at some point, you decided you couldn't live without this." At some point every musician has come to this conclusion, and I hope that the music educators of the future continue to be inspired and driven to continue passing on the knowledge and dedication it takes to make great music. In my book, those who *can* do, teach.

Trusting Your Sound in Performance

Lynn E. Klock

INGREDIENTS:
Preparation and thoughtfulness

SERVES:
All performers.

As performers we are greatly affected by the sound we produce. Rarely do we sound exactly the same in performance as we do in rehearsal. Whether that is caused by adrenaline, nervousness that doesn't allow us to breathe as well, or the different acoustic that results from people being in the audience, there is no doubt that most of the time there is a difference between rehearsal and performance. There are times when we sound better in performance, but this recipe is going to address our reaction as performers to the times when we don't.

I remember performances where I was surprised and greatly disappointed by the sounds I was producing. Unfortunately, my reaction while performing was to question why I hadn't prepared better, and specifically, why I hadn't done a better job of selecting reeds that would have allowed me to play well. This negative energy certainly didn't help the performance. Fortunately, early in my career, I had the chance to listen to recordings of performances where I thought I did not sound good. After listening to the recording, my reaction to myself was "What was your problem?"

The reality is that I sounded quite good, and that all of the negative thoughts and energy were a complete waste of time. My preparation guaranteed that I would sound good, even when the feedback to my ears didn't give me immediate verification. Trust your preparation, because the integrity of your work always shows in performance. ➼

Difference-Maker Tonic

Charles E. Lawson

Given the opportunity, I always ask great players, "How did you get so good?" Their answers contribute to my pedagogical list of performance "difference makers."

The first such experience I remember, was when at age twelve, I asked Rafael Mendez (trumpet virtuoso), "How did you get so good?" His simple answer was, "Practice six hours a day." I said, "Oh," and tried it. Big Difference!

Some years later, during an interview with Karl Leister (former principal clarinetist with the Berlin Philharmonic), he asked me why it took so long for Americans to learn to play. I asked him what he meant, and he compared our junior high through college curriculum with his own experience of beginning clarinet lessons at age fourteen and landing his first symphony job at age seventeen. I immediately asked what he did during those three years. His simple answer was that he played through the Baermann *Complete Method* every day, before practicing something new. This would be comparable to playing the Klosé *Complete* each day!

Reflecting on observations for the past forty-five years reveals many "difference makers." Some are easily observed by the student because results are almost immediate, while others may never be observed by the student because they may never carry out the task. For instance, when a student prepares a solo performance for "Solo and Ensemble Contest," the positive effects are noticed during preparation and immediately after the performance. That same student may never experience the benefits of some of the more intensive long-term commitments, such as practicing "six hours a day." One of my pedagogical goals is to help students experience the benefits of both short- and long-term commitments. Even if the student doesn't maintain the life-long practice habit of a professional performer necessary for technique at that level, the benefits of on perception and musicianship are significant and lasting.

INGREDIENTS:
First the student must have equal parts of the following:
- fascination with sound
- passion for expression with sound
- love of great music
- faith that persistent effort will pay off

Here are some of my favorite short-term "difference makers." Add your own items to the following list:

Preparing a solo performance, especially a memorized performance.
Participating in a chamber ensemble and preparing performances.
Participating in an honor/all-state band or orchestra weekend.
Participating in a summer music camp, especially one that lasts for several weeks.

One long-term "difference maker" that might be missed by the student, if not for the dedication of both student and teacher, is the daily practice of scales and arpeggios. Once a student learns *all* of the major and minor scales and arpeggios, and continues to play them *all* as part of a daily routine, there is a tremendous spike in overall technical achievement at the end of about four months of persistence. I have never seen it to fail, and at the same time I am always pleasantly surprised and amazed with the results. Of course not all students do the work, but for those who do, the change is significant. It really doesn't even have to take much time out of the daily practice session to keep these patterns part of a daily practice routine, yet such a long-term habit pays dividends of increased perception and performance skill, and provides a vehicle for life-long learning.

The following considerations are vital for optimum success:

Play the scale and arpeggio full range and full tone. Since the clarinet has different fingerings in each octave for the same pitch name, the *whole* instrument needs to be practiced. For my students I start by defining "full" range as low E up to high G or G-sharp. For the simple full-range scale, start on the lowest tonic, go up the scale to the highest root, 3rd, or 5th in the range, come back down to as low as possible, and back up to the starting point. There is an adjustment to the range with the lowest note so that the last tonic ends up on the beat. The only top-note adjustment that I routinely make is for the E scales. In order to come out rhythmically in groups of four, it is necessary to go up to high F-sharp (not root, 3rd, or 5th).

Play the patterns in a well-controlled rhythmic ratio of notes per beat. I usually play four notes per beat on the scale and two notes per beat on the arpeggio. A critical error is made when the player is not controlling rhythm. In my early years of teaching, I often overlooked this problem, because the student would play the scale evenly, and I would superimpose my own rhythmic groupings. The student was simply playing a large "glissando" by rote, which sounded good, but ultimately useless when the technique was applied to a composition.

Use a metronome, and tap your foot. The metronome is not a "crutch." Use it your whole life. Tapping the foot and moving the fingers in strict rhythm is a eurhythmic experience, which is vital to rhythmic development.

Once the scale can be played well at a slow tempo, work for speed. Pay attention to hand position and condition. The position is one of efficiency, and the condition is perceived as completely relaxed. As long as the flow of notes is even and relaxation is maintained, keep increasing the metronomic speed. As soon as tension is noticed, slow back down to a tempo in which total relaxation is again felt. Over time the player will enter a dimension of playing and perception that is quite different than playing slowly. Speeds on the easier scales should eventually reach four notes per beat at 200 beats per minute. Aim for routinely playing all of the scales at four notes per beat at 120 beats per minute. Conversely, slow scales are always beneficial for control of all aspects of performance, tone quality, intonation, evenness, etc.

There many, many more observations I could make, but this is a start. For the student intending on majoring in music at the university level, preparing these patterns as part of a daily routine before college would be an excellent plan.

I prefer the harmonic minor scale because it offers the fingers the augmented second, not found in the major or other forms of minor. If the reader would like a complete copy of these patterns, e-mail me at <charles.lawson@colostate.edu>.

SERVES:
Performers by providing a major portion of a life-long practice routine, helping them to benefit to develop brain, fingers, tone, articulation, and pitch. ➦

Developing the Independent Studio

Kenneth Lee

INGREDIENTS:
A motivating teacher
As many students as that teacher can motivate
A viable teaching location
Referrals to get the studio started
Results to build reputation
Preparation time
Frequently, up to five years

SERVES:
Band directors, conductors, the community, students, parents, and the teacher.

Most independent studio music teachers begin their studios wishing they had more practical knowledge and experience to rely upon. As much as we differ as individuals and as teachers, however, it's pretty safe to say that one size won't fit all. Nonetheless, after thirty-five years of honing my independent clarinet studio, I'm going to offer a few suggestions for consideration.

As in any teaching endeavor, our greatest gratification will be the result of inspiring the individual student. There is simply no system or structure that can compare to a charismatic teacher lighting a fire within a flammable student. At the precollege level however, the student who begins lessons with a real personal commitment to her musical studies is very rare. The awakening of the idea that the possibility exists that daily focused practice could lead to something exciting and wonderful is, therefore, job number 1.

To accomplish this objective, I recommend establishing a required daily practice routine. In the early stages this routine needs to take a very short time—perhaps less than 10 minutes. It must first focus the student's mind—no easy task these days. I find a metronome and mirror invaluable in this respect. I try to address one major fundamental at a time—starting with breathing in a four-beat pattern while watching for evidence of diaphragmatic life and a minimum of shoulder movement in the mirror.

Next for me is embouchure development. I find that "modeling" (as Leon Russianoff used the idea) works best. The student takes the mouthpiece out of his mouth and looks at the embouchure formation in the mirror, then strives to maintain it while playing. This "Embouchure Flex Freeze" is an isometric exercise that can develop a focused tone in a rapid enough way to get the student's attention.

An articulation study that involves minimizing the tongue's pressure/contact with the reed and the distance the tongue moves away from the reed is next on the agenda. I like the "tongue tickler" idea of maintaining a tone with the tip of the tongue lightly touching the reed. The position of the hands and the smooth movement of curved fingers landing where they ought to be is next in my short daily warm-up.

As with any system or structure of practice in music, focused attention on both how we play and how we sound are essential for improvement. As the student becomes accustomed to the warm-up routine, I have to continually make it more sophisticated or redirect attention to important aspects now forgotten or over-looked. What we do not inspect will not get the practice attention it requires. It is also true that the warm-up routine that does not evolve in sophistication and in the quality of results expected will cease to be of any value to the student, and will, therefore, not be practiced.

In order to develop the level of the studio as a whole, I have developed clearly defined levels in scales, arpeggios, studies, duets, and theory. My students' progress is displayed on large corkboard wall charts in the studio, by school grade level, in each of the categories above. To indicate the number of years of study, I use different colored nametags so as to not compare, for example, a first-year student with a third-year student in the same grade without recognizing the difference of two years' study. I find that establishing a sort of "at-grade-level" expectation has raised the overall facility level in my studio.

I believe that to develop young musicians' skills requires the acquisition of fluency in both playing and recognizing our most common musical idioms of scales and arpeggios. I try to see that all my students think in the key of the piece and have expectations of (at least) tonic and dominant usages when playing tonal music. I believe that teaching by rote is insulting to the student and mind numbing to the teacher. Teaching comprehension requires longer lessons, but at least there is a cumulative effect.

I believe with all my heart that the instruction I provide is worth what I charge. If I am successful in my teaching, the individual student acquires a sense of what he can accomplish with focused, sustained effort, an appreciation of one of the great art forms of our civilization, and perhaps a bit of the excitement of one of the most wonderful of the performing arts. ➤●

Playing the Contrabassoon

Lewis Lipnick

INGREDIENTS:
A good bassoonist with the willingness to broaden horizons

SERVES:
Orchestras, bassoonists, and the listening public.

Like most contrabassoonists, I started out by playing the "regular" bassoon. It wasn't until I entered eleventh grade of high school at the Interlochen Arts Academy in the fall of 1962 that I became interested in "this instrument that almost always sounded like more of a gastric disturbance than a *musical* instrument." Although I really studied only the bassoon for the two years that I spent at IAA, and the four years I studied for my bachelor of music degree at the Peabody Conservatory, I continued my fascination with the "contra."

It wasn't until I won the position of second bassoon in the National Symphony Orchestra in 1969, and then moved over (via mutual consent within our section) to the "official" contrabassoonist, did I begin to realize that the contrabassoon was a far more difficult instrument to play *well* than the bassoon. Like the tenor or baritone sax, it is very easy to make a "noise" on the contra, but to play it well takes a great deal of air control, physical stamina, good ear training, and, even more than the bassoon, great reeds.

Why is this the case? While I do not consider myself to be an expert in the acoustical dynamics of the contrabassoon, I believe that since the contra has an inherent lower threshold of resistance than the bassoon, clarity of pitch and obtaining a focused sound is more of a challenge. I often joke to my NSO bassoon section colleagues that whenever we are playing a work requiring bassoon and contra doubling, the bassoon seems like a child's toy in difficulty in comparison to the "out of control beastly contra."

So now that I have stated the obvious, how does one go about making a successful transition from bassoon to contrabassoon playing? I believe the "secret" lies in two areas. First, one has to learn to hear pitches *and* the resulting harmonics of those pitches that do not exist on the bassoon. Most German system contras have a very strong "12th" (octave and a fifth above the fundamental). As an example, when I play a contra C (opening solo note of Richard Strauss' *Also Sprach Zarathustra*), I know that I am really "nailing" the pitch center when I can detect a very strong G (octave and a fifth above the contra C). Perhaps that is why Strauss scored the opening of this work for such an odd combination of organ pedal without any octave couplings above sub-contra C (which is a pitch no human can detect), string bass section playing a tremolo contra C (which is not also clearly heard as a distinct low pitch), and contrabassoon playing a sustained contra C. Without the contra, there is virtually no pitch definition to those opening four bars of the piece. But as soon as the contra is added, the audience can immediately identify what they *think* is a contra C. But in fact, it is the G, an octave and a fifth above that C, that tricks their "ears" into "believing" that they are hearing a note that really is not there.

The second most important aspect of contrabassoon playing that I believe makes the difference between a full, resonant sound with clear pitch, and one that sounds like the proverbial case of lower intestinal indigestion, is the psychology of how the air source is directed into the instrument. Please note that I mention *directed into the instrument* and not *through the instrument*. What are we really doing when we play *any* wind instrument? Are we simply trying to displace a huge amount of air into and through the instrument, or are we attempting to acoustically *excite* the air column *within* the instrument? I vote for the latter approach, although an ingoing air source of more volume and speed can indeed make for a louder and more resonant sound.

So now that we have that concept down, let's look at the *main differences* between the proper direction of the air source of the bassoon and the contrabassoon. Since the bassoon inherently has more resistance, we can blow more or less directly into the instrument (assuming that the reed is properly adjusted and is not too hard or soft, etc.). But this just does not work on the contra. I tell my students to think of "spinning" the air column going into the contra, rather than blowing "straight" into the instrument. At first, they don't understand this, and start out sounding worse than they did before. But as soon as I use mind images, such as "think of the contra as a huge hollow log, which you need to get to resonate." Now the student begins to get the idea that if they simply try to blow a lot of air into this "huge log," they will quickly run out of breath and the sound will sound more like they are blowing down a giant sewer pipe than into a woodwind instrument. But when I finally get them to use mind visualization of "spinning a very large air column *into* the instrument, as if the sound were going in a spiral," then the sound comes alive, the pitch becomes more focused, and the student discovers that they have actually expended *less air and energy* than before. Of course, this is an oversimplification of this process, but it works every time.

Thus ends my short dissertation on what I believe to be two of the most important aspects required to obtain a good, focused sound with clear pitch on the contrabassoon. I could easily write another five or six pages on more advanced aspects of contrabassoon performance, and even get into the difference between the dynamics and various designs of contrabassoon reeds vs. those for the bassoon. But I believe that the two points that I have discussed above should help any teacher and student better understand the two main differences between playing the bassoon and playing the contrabassoon. ➤●

Saxophone Recipe Cards: Personal Practice and Performance

Joseph Lulloff

INGREDIENTS:
Personal Preparation, Practice, and Performance

SERVES:
Anyone who plays, teaches, or listens to the saxophone.

Embouchure

Proper embouchure concepts are essential for total control of sound and vibrato. The following are suggestions for forming an embouchure that produces a full, dark, and rich saxophone tone:

> Corners of mouth drawn in
> Lower lip bunched over bottom teeth
> Conceptualize (even vocalize) the word "mew" with this lip formation
> Top teeth placed on top mouthpiece

The proper amount of mouthpiece taken in is important. The top teeth should rest on top center of the mouthpiece at the point where the reed and mouthpiece break away from each other.

The entire embouchure should be firm, hugging the mouthpiece.

Blow a concise and focused air stream into the instrument, focusing the air on a point across the room at eye level.

One should, with the proper embouchure outlined above, be able to produce the following pitches on the mouthpiece alone:

> Soprano Saxophone: concert C (2 octaves above middle C)
> Alto Saxophone: concert A (1 octave and a M6 above middle C)
> Tenor Saxophone: concert G (1 octave and a P5 above middle C)
> Baritone Saxophone: concert E (1 octave and a M3 above middle C)

Breathing: Good Air Equals Good Sound

The following ingredients, combined with proper embouchure, are factors in creating a beautiful saxophone sound:

> Start with good posture.
> Wear loose-fitting, comfortable clothing.

Visualize your breath and your sound.

Strive to relax your body completely before taking a breath.

Breathe in as deeply and quickly (with a relaxed midsection) as you can. Think of saying the word "how" as you inhale.

As you fill your lungs with air, relax your shoulders and relax/expand your midsection.

Practice patterned breathing exercises, both with and without the saxophone.

Exhale as much as you can before taking another breath. Stale air is as bad as an insufficient quantity of air.

Plan and mark your breaths in your music as you practice. Consider musical phrasing, harmonic and melodic content. Listening to recordings of accomplished saxophonists perform the piece in question may help you decide on a breath game plan.

Focus your air as you blow.

Exercise and classes in yoga can be of great benefit to improving one's breathing control and capacity.

Finger Technique

Keep fingers slightly curved.

Place fingertips as directly over the pearls of the saxophone as possible.

Fingers should be a natural extension of the instrument.

Hands should form around the instrument in a relaxed fashion, as if holding a small grapefruit or foam Nerf ball. The fingers and thumb should form a shape of the letter C.

Good technique involves as little finger movement as possible, especially in fast technical passages.

Strive for fingertip contact to the middle of each pearl.

As a rule, use a metronome for about 90 percent of your practice to attain not only good rhythm, but concise and controlled finger motion.

Articulation

Proper articulation involves using an appropriate amount of tongue in contact with the reed, the proper placement of the tongue on the reed, and a thoughtfully sequential procedure in creating the sound. My advice for clear and precise articulation involves:

- Placing the tongue (upper part, just behind the tip) on the reed at a point or area just behind the tip. Close the reed by lightly pressing the tongue against the reed.
- Creating a pressured air base by blowing into the mouthpiece with the tongue closing the reed.
- Releasing the tongue from the reed, conceptualizing the syllable "Da" or La" in order to initiate the sound.
- Stopping the sound by reversing the steps—replacing the same part of the tongue to the same part of the reed.

The smaller the instrument, the lighter stroke that one should use in tonguing. The use of syllables to define certain articulation styles such as accents, *staccato* and *legato*, *marcato*, and similar markings is an excellent way to develop and perfect one's flexibility of articulation on the instrument.

Vibrato

Listen to professional singers, string performers, and wind players to develop your concept and style.

Remain physically relaxed, and concentrate on the movement of the jaw at the hinge.

Conceptualize the syllable syllable "wa or va" to create your vibrato. If this is done, the other muscles will only show visible signs of movement at the point where the lower lip meets the mouthpiece.

Do not create the vibrato above the pitch. A vibrato that undulates between slightly below the pitch to the center of the pitch, with a smooth curve (sine wave) at all times, will develop into a spinning vibrato over time.

Begin slowly, using the metronome to guide the development of your vibrato speed. Use the following guide, only progressing until the vibrato wave becomes unsteady. Stop, and work at that tempo and below until you gain consistency, then move onward.

Start with: quarter note=60, making one cycle per beat, and increase the metronome speed to 120.

Continue at quarter note=60 with two cycles per beat, gradually increasing the metronome speed to 100.

Continue at quarter note=60 with three cycles per beat, gradually increasing the metronome speed to 90.

Continue at quarter note=60 with four cycles per beat, gradually increasing the metronome speed to 88.

In the end, spin the vibrato to achieve the most singing quality possible.

Practice Habits

A structured warm-up pattern and a structured practice schedule is important. Students with a background of a structured practice environment can bring an element of preparation and professionalism to any group. Moreover, *slow practice* and *silent practice* of several aspects of music is key to a successful performance. From developing technical skills of vibrato, articulation, and technique to working out stylistic decisions of interpretation—these two types of practice techniques can prove to be extremely effective. Plan enough time to cover each of the following areas in your practice sessions:

- Long tones and slow intervallic warm-up exercises
- Overtone and voicing exercisers
- Technical study (scales and technical patterns that cover both the normal and the extended altissimo range, articulation exercises, etc.)
- Etude work for both musical, technical, and stylistic study
- Repertoire works that cover at least two styles or periods of composition
- Playing through works that you studied in the past for your own enjoyment
- Long tones for warming-down exercises
- Daily listening to recordings of both saxophone and non-saxophonists to develop one's own tonal and stylistic concept of all areas of musical performance is essential.

Recording Practice Sessions/Concerts and Marking Parts

Recording parts of your practice session can be beneficial to see how you sound from the "outside." Listening to your recording and marking individual parts with cues of rhythmic figures and other hints can bring to light many performance issues that often go unnoticed until it is too late. Listen for tonal clarity and consistency throughout your range, for intonation throughout the instrument's range, for clarity of articulation, and, if playing with ensemble, for overall balance, blend, intonation, and rhythmic accuracy. Recording concerts can tell you how you do in a pressure situation and through careful study and creative thinking, you can implement practice techniques that will quickly solve your performance issues.

Listening

It is imperative for young saxophonists to develop fine listening skills, especially of works or styles that they are currently studying. Consistent listening will aid in developing a solid basic sound concept for the musician. Research of Internet Web sites of various collegiate saxophone studios throughout the nation will lead to listening lists for a variety of saxophone repertoire and styles. These sites will also have information on where to purchase saxophone CDs or tracks of saxophone music. These sites provide an excellent resource for classical, contemporary, and jazz saxophone music. ➞●

Basic Woodwind Instrument Care

Bruce Marking

An integral part of playing an instrument is making sure the instrument is playable at all times. Here are simple suggestions and practical steps for you and your students that can increase reliability of the instruments and reduce repair costs for your program.

INGREDIENTS:
Basic tools for woodwind instruments:
small screwdriver
swab
key oil and needle
handkerchief

SERVES:
All instrumental teachers and students.

I still remember my junior high band director telling us how to take care of our instruments. I even remember his description of giving the brass instruments a "bath," even though I play the clarinet! I don't remember a time in public school band when many people complained about a nonfunctioning instrument or having the local repair person taking multiple instruments away for repair each week. I believe that with a few basic tools and minimal skill, teachers and students can keep their instruments in good shape and playable at all times.

Basic Woodwind Instrument Care
Before assembling the instrument for each playing session, inspect the instrument for broken or missing corks and, especially, loose screws and rods. Use the screwdriver on the loose screws. The mechanism should be oiled every two or three months. A bottle of key oil will last your entire life, if used properly. Place a *small* amount of oil on a needle or pin (*do not apply oil directly from the bottle!*) and apply it to the pivot points of the keys. The pivot point is located between the end of the hinge tube of the key and the post on the body of the instrument. If you put too much oil on the key, use a cloth to wipe off the excess. Keep the oil off the pads. Use a soft brush to occasionally remove the dust and dirt from under the keys. Use cork grease on the joint corks if you have difficulty assembling the instrument. Do not use grease on flute joints. Check to see that all the springs are in place on the keys. It is easy to push most needle springs back into place for proper operation of the key. Some flat springs may break, but sometimes they just come loose from the key and can be tightened easily. These small repairs take almost no time and can save a day or a week without the instrument.

Assemble woodwind instruments carefully, especially flutes, clarinets, and oboes. Hold the parts of the instrument in each hand and *gently twist* them together. If you set the bottom of the joint in the case in your lap and push the top joint down into it, you run the risk of breaking the middle tenon. I prefer to assemble my clarinet from the bottom up, placing the delicate reed on the instrument last, *through the ligature*, minimizing the risk of damaging the tip of the reed!

One of the most important things a woodwind player can do to keep the instrument in good condition is to *swab the bore*, and much more frequently than you may think! I recommend swabbing in long rests, between movements, between pieces, at intermission, and at the end of each performance, rehearsal, or practice session. This may seem excessive, but anyone who has experienced gurgling or nonresponsive notes during a performance knows that it's much better to use the swab than to risk the frustration! When finished with a playing session you should also dry the sockets and ends of the tenons. Swab the mouthpiece about once a week, to minimize wear of the critical rail edges. Anyone who has looked in the bore of a dirty clarinet or flute, or particularly a clarinet or saxophone mouthpiece that hasn't *ever* been swabbed, knows that it isn't pretty. I suggest that players *at least* rinse their mouths with water before playing, if it isn't practical to use a toothbrush.

I have had saxophone players come in with the complaint that the neck receiver wouldn't tighten. Usually it was because the screw had been removed and replaced backwards. The receiver is a clamp and is threaded only on one side. If the screw is in backwards, it will not pull together to hold the neck. Saxophones should be swabbed, just like flutes, oboes, and clarinets.

The guard screws on saxophones should be tightened regularly. These screws should be examined upon assembly of the instrument each time. Loose guards can rattle and cause the mechanism to operate improperly. They protect the keys from bumps and loose clothing.

Some people have problems with hand and finger pain because of playing a woodwind instrument. Saxophone players should always use a neck strap. I also believe, with the perspective of a clarinet player, that saxophone players use improper hand position. Often I see the neck of the saxophone lined up with the bell, which tends to twist the hands improperly. I think the neck should be lined up with the thumb rest, which puts the keys forward, and the hands straight. The mouthpiece often gets twisted to line up vertically with the body of the saxophone. This causes the player's head to lean if the instrument is played on the side. I always tell students to "make the instrument fit them." It is easy with a saxophone, because of the adjustability of the neck and the mouthpiece. These may seem to be minor considerations, but little things add up. For a player who may be spending many hours practicing and performing, there can be tragic consequences.

Oboe and clarinet players are constricted by the position of the thumb rest on the instrument as it comes from the factory. Usually it is mounted too low, which forces the thumb downward. This position automatically causes problems. The leverage of the weight of the instrument on the thumb (already at a disadvantage because of the downward angle) causes pain and discomfort, especially for beginning students. If you grab something, take notice of how your thumb is in opposition to your index finger. You can get a technician to raise the thumb rest on your instrument to match this position. Even adjustable thumb rests tend to be mounted to low on the body of the instrument. They can be moved upward as well.

Good instrument care habits are just as important as good practice and performance habits. Incorporate regular instrument inspections into your program. Grading periods are automatic intervals that can be used. Give students a checklist (with enough time to have major repairs done) during each period. Plan inspection times for efficiency and fit in your program. You may divide the time by woodwind and brass, by section, by instrument, or whatever is convenient. A student *with* an instrument is learning, contributing, and enjoying the musical experience. *Without* an instrument they are bored and can be discipline problems. Having all instruments in working condition allows the group to improve constantly and with less stress and distraction. Enjoy the music! ➤●

Rich Tone Production with Centered Pitch à la Whistle Tones

Leslie Marrs

Whistle tones (also known as whisper tones, flageolets) have been used by flutists for years to enhance embouchure placement and development as well as breath control. Side benefits include increased pitch awareness, greater comfort playing in the fourth octave of the flute, amazing your friends, and confounding your enemies, cats, and birds.

INGREDIENTS:
One or more flutists, with flutes in hand, and a sense of adventure

SERVES:
Flutists, composers, and their audiences.

Wind players in general have special issues in tone production because most aspects of the embouchure are hidden from view. The shape of the oral cavity, and tongue and teeth positions are invisible to the observer and are further obscured by the presence of a mouthpiece directly in front of the lips. Flutists in particular have special issues due to the fact that 1) unlike other wind performers, the mouthpiece comes in contact with only the lower lip during regular tone production and 2) unlike other woodwind players, there is no reed to guide tonguing. Almost all tone deficiencies in flute playing are the result of the position of the embouchure (lips, tongue, and oral cavity) and/or airflow. William Kincaid (1895-1967), renowned pedagogue and principal flutist with the Philadelphia Orchestra (1921-1960), advocated producing these delicate sounds as a method of eliminating deficiencies and improving sound.

A teacher or conductor may observe that a flute student has an acceptable but not wonderful sound. There may be some sonic fuzz present, and perhaps flexibility is limited due to some aspect of the tone. This could be the result of a flattened tongue position, teeth close together, and/or the lips may be pulled back too tightly or too relaxed. Having the flutist whistle can pave the road to solving this dilemma. In order to whistle, the teeth need to be open about a finger's width, the tongue needs to be arched in back, and the lips need to be forward.

Ask the player to whistle and take note of one or all of these aspects, then apply them to flute playing. *Note that the flute embouchure is not quite as far forward as the average whistling lip position.

If the player is unable to whistle, have him or her say "eee" on the inside of the mouth while bringing the lips around to say "ooo." The resulting vowel should sound like the French "u" sound in the words "tu" and "flûte" (a layering of "i/u"). This usually results in the same position as whistling.

Have the flutist play a note in a comfortable range, then whistle or sing the pitch on "û" (an octave away is okay). Keep this position for the next step.

Return the flute to this improved embouchure. Blow slow, warm air across the embouchure plate. Strive for a light, whispery sound that resembles a teakettle whistle. *If a regular flute tone or only air sounds, practice this slower air stream by blowing onto the index finger close to the lips. This warm/hot air stream should leave moisture on the finger. Return to producing a whistle tone; repeat playing and singing a pitch as needed.

If there is difficulty reproducing the exact pitch fingered, hold any whistle tone steady and strive for at least 8 seconds. As the comfort level with this technique increases, hone the whistle tone production so that it is possible to echo the original flute tone with a whistle tone of the same pitch.

Even if the student is incapable of producing a whistle tone, the awareness of the above three aspects of embouchure—oral cavity, tongue, and lip positions—will open the door to improved tone production. A sense of adventure and experimentation with the above steps will lead the student to the ability to produce whistle tones.

The end result in flute sound is a more focused sound, with a rich and open quality that lends itself to ease of flexibility in range, dynamics, and tone color. Playing a steady whistle tone for at least 8 seconds demands an absolutely steady air stream. Whistle tones may be quiet, but they have amazing projection. This brings new perspective to regular flute playing: it is not necessary to blow forcefully to produce a clear, projecting tone. In addition, a steady air stream is the foundation for refining breath control. Since flute tone production is defined by a split air column—some air goes into the flute and some does not—breathing management is the only way to fly on the flute. This is training every flutist should add to their regimen.

As the flutist develops the ability to produce precise pitches, pitch awareness is internalized and enhanced. Whistle tones are wonderful for learning high notes on the flute. High A (A6; third octave A on the flute) is a favorite place of mine to introduce students to whistle tones. As they learn notes in to the fourth octave, playing them as whistle tones instead of regular tones will allow the flutist to get the pitches "in their ears" while learning the fingerings—without taxing the embouchure muscles. Familiarity with the fingerings allows them to play scales and musical passages that contain high pitches and concentrate on tone rather than finger dexterity. The range of playable whistle tones on the flute is from about low A (A4) up through pitches in the fourth octave. Care must be taken with lower (first octave) whistle tones, so that the tongue does not cause constriction of the airflow. There *can* be too much of a good thing, and each person should decide where the comfort zone boundary lies.

Playing whistle tones as echoes of pitches yields incredible **fppp** effects. While composers may wish to include this technique in a composition for musical purposes, flutists may find this type of echoing a good personal model for **fppp** in regular flute production. It is also possible to play the overtone series on whistle tones. This advanced step in whistle tone technique further enhances pitch awareness and embouchure development.

The unassuming whistle tone allows for great benefits in many aspects of flute playing, as a certain flick of the wrist would improve sautéing, kneading dough, or whisking batter or sauce in cooking. As this technique is perfected, there's the added angle of amazing your friends and confounding the uninitiated! ➝●

Developing a Flexible Oboe Embouchure

James Mason

Of all the ingredients that combine to make a successful oboist, a flexible embouchure is probably the most important. You can have the most incredible posture, a well-developed air speed, and fabulous finger dexterity, and still not sound good if you have an embouchure that doesn't allow for adjustment and control. Ironically, a well-developed flexible embouchure enhances all of the aforementioned attributes. Let's get cooking!

INGREDIENTS:

A reed that speaks easily is desirable.

An oboe that is in good mechanical repair is essential. Most oboes work well if there is a minimum hold of 20 seconds of suction on the top joint and 10 seconds of suction on the bottom joint. In my opinion, the Yamaha YOB841 model is the most responsive. To check for suction, take the joint in question and close all the keys with the appropriate hand. With the free hand, cover one end of the joint with a finger (or, in the case of the bottom joint, use the heel of the thumb) and suck on the other end. Count how long the joint holds the suction. I know that, because of the expense of instrument maintenance and the budget of most high school and university students, these numbers are a luxury. However, the improvement that a student can make with an instrument that works properly is incredibly gratifying and rewarding for both student and teacher. Low notes are much easier to play and are better in tune. Descending slurs over the break (most critically from any notes above fourth line D to A, A-flat, G or F-sharp in the staff) work more fluidly. Most importantly, the entire instrument "rings" more when played at any dynamic level.

A student with patience and who is willing to work.

A tuner. I'll say more about this later.

SERVES:

Everyone: the player, his/her colleagues, the conductor, the audience, friends (who don't have to put up with the oboist's whining), parents (who don't have to put up with the oboist's whining), etc. You get the picture.

Without putting the reed in the oboe, place the reed on the bottom lip and form the embouchure around the reed. When I say "around the reed," I mean exactly that. You should think of imitating a whistle or a kiss, and then just invert the lips. Your chin should be pointing down and your oral cavity should be forming the vowel sound "ah." Pressure from the embouchure should be fairly equal all the way around the reed. Now, while imagining playing a middle register note at a mezzo forte volume, blow a note on the reed. You should produce a pitch that is somewhere between an A-natural and a B-flat. If your pitch is too high, put less reed in your mouth. Now, play that note again, forte this time, and make a diminuendo. The pitch should not go up. Try it again with a tuner, if possible. This time hold the note out for a longer period of time, experimenting with the lip muscles, trying to find what works to keep the pitch the same. Being able to successfully perform this exercise on a regular basis is the goal that we are trying to achieve.

After practicing this exercise on the reed alone and becoming fairly proficient at maintaining the pitch, you are now ready to try it on the oboe. Pick a note to start with that is relatively stable. Usually fourth-line D is a good choice. Take a good breath and play, starting the sound with a "tah" articulation. As in the first exercise, your chin should be down from the beginning of the articulation. At no time should your articulation be "tee-ah." Start at a pianissimo volume and make a crescendo to fortissimo and then diminuendo back to pianissimo. Do this over a nine-beat period, starting with pianissimo being level 1, making a crescendo to level 5, which is fortissimo, then making a diminuendo back to level 1.

You will be, in essence, playing the following exercise: 1(pp), 2, 3, 4, 5(ff), 4, 3, 2, 1(pp). This is called a *long tone*, and is probably the most useful exercise that the oboist can perform. It can be performed in several different ways. You can slur as in the manner that I just described. You can lightly articulate each level. As you advance you can play on more levels of gradation (i.e. 1–7–1 or 1–9–1, etc.). Eventually you will come to see that this exercise is not only designed for dynamics. It also enhances your ability to create and control tone color.

I can't think of any time in my career where the ability to perform long tones hasn't enhanced what I was trying to do on the oboe. Once you understand how the embouchure works with your air column to produce the long tone, start practicing the exercise over the full range of the oboe. You will find that the practicing of long tones helps develop all aspects of your ability to make music, as well as your embouchure: tone, endurance, control, articulation, and, yes, even your technique. Practicing long tones in the upper register really helps build tone and control in a range of the instrument that is notorious for sounding "thin" in the wrong hands. Low register long tones really improve the ability to play those difficult low notes that the oboe is infamous for. Long tones improve the embouchure so you can articulate notes of any length at any dynamic, since all that practice of playing on the tip of the reed eliminates the need to feel as if you have to "hold on" to the reed, thus causing you to slow down.

One caution in closing: while practicing with a tuner can be beneficial, don't let it allow your eyes to become your ears. In other words, use the tuner as a reference, not a guide. There will be a temptation to look at the tuner while playing and adjusting pitch by what you see instead of what you hear. A better idea would be to get a colleague to watch the tuner in order to confirm or contradict what you thought you heard. Enjoy the journey! ➾

Connections

Steve McNeal

INGREDIENTS:
Intelligence and the desire for excellence

SERVES:
Generations of students.

As a woodwind (WW) player and a public school orchestra director/teacher, I discovered the possibilities of "connections" to help the full orchestra.

On the one hand:
When a director stays in the orchestra room, totally involved in his/her own string world, full orchestra potential becomes closed or shut out. Isolation may be a "safe" but unhealthy retreat. China, as an aggressive, inventive society, closed out the world, keeping their knowledge to themselves by building the Great Wall. They were safe; no one could find out their secrets. The disastrous result of their choice was that they were isolated. New ideas couldn't get in, and new ideas couldn't get out. Similarly, orchestra teachers may find themselves isolated, closed, stuck, safe, and very lonely.

And on the other hand:
The band directors/colleagues I taught with all recognized and valued the importance of the orchestra experience for their wind and percussion players. When I offered my skills to help their students, our relationships prospered. I opened connecting doors by asking these questions of my band director/colleague: "What may I do to help?" "Are there two to three things I may do to make your job go better?" "Are there several WW players I could help?" "I would like to get to know the students in your band." I found that by offering assistance, a likewise response greeted me. I was fortunate to have band directors who supported the orchestra. I have observed situations where the band director didn't want a full orchestra in the school; consequently, there wasn't one. When the band director acknowledges the value of the symphony orchestra, there will be a full symphony orchestra in the school.

Your community, administrators, and staff must be in agreement about the overall necessity of having basic things in place.

Scheduling suggestions:
Advanced band and orchestra meet during the same class period in two separate rooms.

Classes meet daily: String rehearsal is three days a week or M, W, F. Full band is scheduled three days a week or M, W, F. (Block scheduling require some variation of this.)

Full orchestra then meets T, TR. (The orchestra winds and percussion may be auditioned. When the directors know their students, another effective way of choosing the players for full orchestra is a collaborative decision by the two directors. The following aspects may be considered: ability, grade level, maturity, skill level, potential, etc.)

This schedule is followed throughout the year. As important events approach, it is important for the two directors to adjust the rehearsal time to accommodate necessary extra rehearsal time.

Benefits:

The advanced players selected or chosen for full orchestra develop more independent playing characteristics.

The wind and percussion students tend to develop soloistic performing qualities.

The students in band and not selected for full orchestra receive more attention.

The advanced wind and percussion students in band and full orchestra experience a wider variety of music.

For the enhancement of community, on the one hand:

A philosophy of "community" instilled in a music ensemble enhances a music department and consequently the overall environment of a school. A nurturing, mutually supportive, family-like environment develops confidence and a wholesome atmosphere for students to comfortably learn and grow. When the extremely competitive approach of a musical ensemble is minimized, more may be accomplished.

For the minimization of competition, on the other hand:

Students who have the skills and who wish to compete may be encouraged to audition for all-state honor groups, summer camps, local youth orchestras, etc. to compete against students from other schools. This approach lends itself to students within individual schools supporting one another, rather than competing aggressively against each another. There will always be an element of competition. The more it can be minimized and an alternative realized, the better the environment may become.

The woodwind orchestra teacher:

Having skills with WW instruments and being able to express them verbally in the orchestra rehearsal may help instill confidence in the entire ensemble. The WW player/teacher may use his/her knowledge, experience, and skill of playing to connect with the full orchestra. Performing any literature in any ensemble demands more from us than just getting the notes and rhythms. From early contact with the students in the school year, the director may ask much more than the notes. It is exciting to teach WW instruments in the setting of a school orchestra. The following are ideas and examples of ways to say things to help students visualize the changes of sound. Changes in tone color and a rhythmically unified ensemble will quickly enhance the performance of the music being rehearsed.

Tone quality, a few ideas:

Warmth of sound: Open the back of the throat, think of initiating the tone deeper in your body, blow warm air, center the sound.

For a solo line: Fill the room with your sound, put your tone in the back of the room. The player's part may indicate a "p" dynamic, and a young player may simply think "mf." A more advanced player may be able to achieve the desired result by playing a piano dynamic but add breath support intensity under the soft dynamic.

For ensemble playing: Ask the student to think balance and blend. Start with two players then add one at a time, focusing the players' attention as they concentrate on working for balance and blend. Usually just a few specific moments are needed for the students to improve and meet the goal set for them.

Rhythmical clarity:

Repeated rhythms: Being a "motor" for other sections. Clarify the rhythm by emphasizing the beat. In passages with pitch changes students may slightly to and accent or lean on the beat.

Melodic rhythms: Decide where important notes lie in the melody. Meet the director on these important notes in this passage. The director will have opened the door for the students to watch the conductor and listen to others around the ensemble.

Technical difficulties: May combine with rhythmical passages. Suggest to students that they play the passage enough that relaxation rather than tension is felt as they perform. Alternate fingerings may solve problems in some passages.

Choose music carefully:

The music chosen and the inventive ways selected to teach the literature are of utmost importance. The music facilitator/conductor must uphold the highest integrity of the composer's intentions. This is an opportunity to use creativity as we think of the variety of approaches to players and especially the WW section of the orchestra. The use of everyday events brings relevance to music that helps students picture performance possibilities. A homecoming activity may provide the director with a picture to help with a certain passage in a piece on which the ensemble is working. Use the mood that is created when standardized test taking is scheduled. There are lots of places in pieces where this certain feeling may be used to get a desired feeling from a spot in the music. Being aware and using things that occur daily are practical tools of connecting.

Keep things positive:

A positive attitude from the orchestra director toward the wind and percussion players is vital. Young students placed in an orchestra for the first time should be treated as tender young plants. They need time to put down roots. One misplaced or mistimed attitude of anger from a director may ruin a potentially wonderful musician. The strings must learn respect for the orchestra winds and percussion, and, in turn the winds and percussion must learn respect and empathy toward the strings. The daily nurturing needed is almost overwhelming when time is taken to think about it. It is so easy and natural to address issues negatively. Consequently, directors need to train their own minds to take a 180-degree turn and express instructions with a positive twist of words. It takes time to make this a habit, but it gets easier the more it is practiced.

In closing:

There may never be an end to the work involved in developing a wonderful WW section in an orchestra. However, the journey can be a rewarding and wonderful experience for director, students, parents, and a community. Most likely when the WW section is good, other sections will rise to meet the challenge created by the fine WW playing. It has happened before. Set your sights high and never give up. Never! ➤

Recipe for Difference Tones—Develops Pitch Flexibility and Control

Gary Moody

INGREDIENTS:
Two players or one player along with a drone pitch

SERVES:
One and all. Helps to build intonation sensitivity, control, and flexibility.

Select a single note, held steadily. This sound can be accomplished by a person playing, but more easily with an electronic source like a drone from a tuner or a synthesizer. Select a tone that is without vibrato. Allow that sound to be the 5th of a major triad.

Blend well the 3rd of the major triad. Knead the pitch of the 3rd by bending it sharper and flatter while listening for the combination of the two as it renders a buzz in your ear. When seasoned to perfect blend, the root of the triad will appear. This is the difference of the two frequencies. The clearest root will appear with the 3rd played a bit low (fourteen cents) in pitch to equal temperament.

Now blend against the 5th a minor 3rd. Once again knead its pitch while listening. When blended perfectly, it will render the root of a minor triad, and will be clearest when this minor third is played a bit sharp and spicy (sixteen cents high).

Why is this happening? Any two notes sounded together will create a *resultant* or *difference* tone that is the difference of the two frequencies. The eighteenth century violinist Giuseppe Tartini heard these notes as he played double stops and dubbed them "Tartini Tones."

Every natural sound generates harmonics that sound above it. (The harmonic series is shown below up to the sixth harmonic.) The frequencies of these harmonics are all multiples of the fundamental. So if a note has a frequency of "x," the frequencies of the harmonics will be 2x, 3x, etc. If we play two notes that are adjacent notes in the harmonic series of some fundamental, we will create that fundamental (4x-3x=x).

Additionally, these difference tones react with the actual notes to create a second generation of difference tones that will either be sweetly in tune with the harmonics and reinforce the sound, or, if out of tune, create a bitter taste in the aural palate.

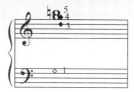

Difference tones are especially valuable because they magnify the pitch variation. Take the interval of a major 3rd, which has the frequency ratio of 5 to 4. Let's pretend that the frequencies of the two notes are 500 and 400 cycles. Their difference is 100 cycles. If we raise the upper note of the interval by 1 percent to 505 cycles, the difference will rise a full 5 percent, and thus magnify the pitch error.

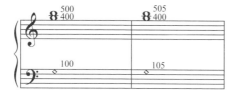

Harmonics need not be adjacent. Any two in a series will create a difference that also lies in that series.

A pair from higher in the series may also be lower numbered harmonics from a higher fundamental.

The harmonic series does not stop at six, but ascends theoretically to infinity. Here is the series through the ninth harmonic. Between each harmonic the size of the interval between it and the note below decreases as the series ascends. There is an octave between the first and second harmonics, a perfect fifth between two and three, a perfect fourth between three and four, a major third between four and five, and a minor third between five and six. The apparent minor third between six and seven is narrower, with the pitch of the seventh harmonic quite low in relation to equal temperament.

If you bend the size of a minor third interval, you can create different fundamentals. A flatter shade of the B-flat mixed with G produces the interval common to the C harmonic series, while a sharper version creates the interval common to the E-flat series.

There is a variety of major second intervals that decrease in size between seven and eight, eight and nine, and again between nine and ten. Bending the placement of the A against the G can create intervals common to different fundamentals. As the interval between the A and G shrinks, the smaller difference creates a lower difference tone.

Playing the following exercises can help tune the ear and build intonation control.

Careful kneading and seasoning will create pitch flexibility, resulting in more tonal colors in the palette, which will serve everyone's aural palate. →•

A Gourmet Kitchen Does Not a Chef Make

Ricardo Morales

INGREDIENTS:
A wind instrument
Scales and arpeggios

SERVES
All wind instrumentalists who care about refinement.

It is disappointing that no matter how fancy my convection oven, my cooking utensils, and my recipe books are, I never manage to cook as well as my mother! She has always cooked with great variety and subtlety, with what can nowadays be assessed as an "average" kitchen, and without my impressive spice depot.

I find great similarity with some our modern woodwind music making, listening to many players with what could be considered a huge technical salad bar, yet with few delicious morsels to be able to assemble a great meal. Using the simplicity principles of my mother's kitchen, let us look at a few steps we can use to improve our technique, and therefore communicate more musically. Let's start cooking!

The most important aspect of acquiring a proficient technique is to be able to apply it to the music we are performing. We all have practiced technical exercises to improve facility, yet I believe it is more important to use those skills to enhance our musical palette.

Scales and arpeggios are two of the most talked about items that are supposed to be used in our technical development. Many players can play them, but not in a musical context. Let us talk about these two basic technical tools and see how we can put them to better use—let's think of them as our salt and pepper.

It is known that scales must be practiced slowly at first, with great attention to intonation, correct fingerings, and finger placement. Once these steps are more familiar, one is to increase speed, octave range, and different articulations for better finger/tongue coordination. One way to "salt to taste" our scales is to put them in the context of what we are cooking—in other words, we must also practice the type of tone we want to have in the particular passage of music we wish to perform. While practicing scales we should try to have a composer or musical style in mind, not just what we call a plain tone, which is seldom used in our musical endeavors. Without focusing on this element, we are often left without a clear, useful way of *performing* scales. Many instrumentalists also get tired or bored of practicing technical exercises because when playing with just an arbitrary or plain tone, it becomes harder to relate those sounds to actual music, therefore adding to the loss of interest in the task at hand.

Arpeggios need similar attention to detail as scales, but we must add an important ingredient. The way to "pepper" our arpeggios is to improve our connections. While practicing slowly, we must concentrate on blending the notes not only with finger coordination and suppleness, but also filling the space between the notes. One way of trying this technique requires two parts. First, we can do a crescendo of air before the next note is played, changing to the note at the top of the crescendo. Secondly, it must be practiced the opposite way, starting with a full tone, playing the next note at the end of the diminuendo. It is critical to be able to connect the notes with similar ease in both exercises, finally getting to the point where the player can maintain evenly the air speed between the notes. One must be mindful of creating homogeneity between the notes in order to avoid unnecessary swells and distortions of musical phrases.

Air should also be used to clarify phrasing, and must have the capability to change musical direction and intensity. In the most basic way, increasing or decreasing the amount of air corresponding to the dynamics intended usually helps with musical shape. Musical intensity can be measured by the speed of air one uses while making adjustments for the different amounts of resistance in between the notes, combined with the volume of air being produced. These two aspects have to be mastered separately, since there are many occasions when the two skills have to be used independently of each other. Speed of air can also change the tonal color that is used, and thus affect the character of the music at hand.

Once we are more comfortable with the use of our salt and pepper, we can build on more complex recipes, and be on our way to create, re-create, and expand on our favorite musical cuisine. *Bon appétit!* ━●

Recipe for Pain-Free Playing

Christine A. Moran

Considering yourself as an athlete is probably the farthest idea from the mind of a musician. A musician considers oneself a musician—an artist. Look at what you do everyday. You use muscles in precise patterns of movement over and over many times. You require excellent response every time. Sounds like an athlete to me.

Do you take the time to prepare your body for practice and performance? Do you take into account how stressful playing is to your upper body?

INGREDIENTS:
Playing posture analysis, gentle stretching, light strengthening, aerobic activity

SERVES:
All wind players.

Playing posture evaluation by a physical therapist/hand therapist with a background in musician treatment can provide much information about how you use you upper body while playing. This evaluation can identify painful or stressful postures that develop during playing. Rather than changing how you play, the evaluation can identify which muscle groups need strengthening to support the arms and hands while playing. The upper back and shoulder muscles are required to hold steady particular positions for endless intervals while the hands manipulate the instrument. What kinds of activities or exercise to you engage in to keep the upper back muscles healthy and toned?

First and foremost, stretch before and after you play. Many studies have demonstrated the helpful benefits of stretching. Blood flow is improved to muscles and tendons. There is improved elasticity of structures that allows easier movement. You actually play longer with less physical discomfort. Don't overextend the joints to stretch muscles; apply the force gently and hold for counts of 5 to 10. No matter your instrument, stretch hands, wrists, shoulders, neck, and upper back. If playing standing, perform easy ballet plies or semi-squats to ease your low back and create flexibility there.

What about your trunk muscles? Yes, those muscles that hold your back and stomach in place. Good posture is necessary for skillful playing. How often do you address those muscles in your daily routine? Exercise, brisk walking, sit-ups. Skillful playing requires that you have good proximal support. These are similar parameters that are known to proponents of Alexander and Feldenkrais techniques.

But how does it happen when you have a job or school and four to five hours of practice? Create space for prevention. Brisk walk with the next piece of music playing on your iPod or Walkman. Create opportunities to exercise while bathing, brushing your teeth, cooking dinner.

Weight lifting is another good addition to your routine. Low weights (under 5 lbs.) with many reps will increase your endurance for performance and keep those muscles toned. Joining a club is not required. Instead, you can use a few free weights or exercise tubing in your home. There are very effective exercises for the upper back that require no equipment.

The cliché of prevention rings true in this scenario. Take the time to have your playing posture evaluated. Receive suggestions for stretching and strengthening . . . Begin a walking program now. All of these suggestions will promote pain-free playing before the important audition or big gig. ➤●

Teaching Technical Issues of the Oboe; Addressed Through Passion, Singing, and Acting

Paige Morgan

INGREDIENTS:

An understanding of basic oboe technique, including tone, fingering, tonguing, pitch, and rhythm

A willingness and desire to share passion and one's own deep expression from within the music

CDs, DVDs of various operas and/or movies

SERVES:

The oboist and all those teaching and listening.

Technical instructions are essential to every musician, regardless of instrument. "Technique," not only in the fingering sense, but in those listed above, has always been the bane of my existence. I have spent much of my life as an oboist separating musicality and technique, one of which I seemed blessed with and one of which I most definitely was not. Fingers, tonguing, rhythm, and reeds frustrated me to no end, but gave me something simple and beautiful to play—and a good reed—and nothing could stop my "musical potential," as so many people always told me. How does one bring out the musical aspects of a piece but do all of the technical things we must be able to do?

It wasn't until I stopped the fracas between these two "opposing" camps and began *using* my passion and musicality to approach everything technical, that my musical life and oboe playing started to make sense. By approaching everything musically, by figuring out the character or mood of a phrase as if I were an opera diva or an actor, the technical issues fell into place.

First, a few basic technical instructions which all oboe players have most likely been given at some point in their lives:

1. **Tone**—form an oval shape with your mouth, so the corners of your mouth are more forward, creating a focused sound; stay close to the tip of the reed in low to mid range—too much reed in the mouth can cause a crass sound; fast air always.
2. **Finger ease**—relax fingers; keep them curved and close to the keys; practice scales in all patterns and tempos; keep working towards more and more difficult etudes.
3. **Tonguing**—relax your tongue; tip of the tongue to the tip of the reed; always have air behind the tongue so all notes will speak.

4. **Pitch**—practice intervals constantly, especially with a drone; train your ear to hear intervals; play with others for ease of adjusting to anyone's pitch.
5. **Rhythm**—keep working to feel the inner beat; practice first with a metronome, then without, and a third time with again; buy a drum book and practice playing various rhythms on one note only; record yourself and while listening back, turn on a metronome, thus pointing out where you went askew.

And the list goes on. All of these are important and necessary, but can be dull and tedious when done without the context of the music.

I now approach everything I play by first figuring out the character and mood of any given phrase in any piece of music. I ask myself, and I have found this most helpful in teaching, to do the following:

1. Take a phrase or entire section or movement from any piece and think about what you believe is happening in the music. What is the character?
2. Put words to the music—anything that pops into your head.
3. If you were an opera singer or actor, what do you think is happening on stage right now? For example, do you sense anger, sadness, joy, irritability, fear, panic, pure love, contemplation? Is it a beautiful, carefree day in the park, are you angry at a friend, are you flirting with someone, did your father just die? While sometimes difficult to determine right away, I have found that all of us can make up something, and attaching it to what we hear in the music is something many musicians do without even thinking about it. Now, play the phrase while thinking about this—really put yourself into the character.

The really wonderful thing I find about this process, again, especially with students, is you just never know what is going to come out of someone's mouth. Some of the most imaginative stories I've ever heard have come from students for whom I wondered if when they stood in line for creativity, they weren't given a number. This has proven to me what I always thought true, that we are all creative, just in so many different ways.

When I put all of this together, when I have my students then play with the story in mind, when I or they imagine a big movie screen with their story taking place to their musical playing, or a diva singer singing whatever they are imagining—at that moment, magical things begin to happen. Fingers relax. The tongue relaxes (unless perhaps they are imaging Stephen King–type images!) Breathing seems easier because where to breath makes more sense, because it fits into the story or character. Rhythm makes more sense because it has a context in which to fit. Tone opens up and students are not nearly as afraid to blow, or to play "brighter" or "darker" depending on how they want to portray the character. They tend to have much more energy in their playing. Most exciting for me is they *enjoy* what they are playing so much more. Barret Melody #19 is no longer simply another exercise; it has purpose, it is fun, and they are more encouraged to practice.

In light of all this, I ask my students to watch various operas. After they have watched them, I ask them, in whatever they are working on in a lesson, what character from that opera do they think they are portraying? If opera doesn't intrigue them as much as it does me, I have them rent any movie they wish, and ask them to think about the music verses the character and story going on at any given moment. I then have them determine something from that movie which is similar to what they are playing.

How do they bring that out in the music? Imagination—imagining they are accompanying the plot, or imitating the mood and character, right there with their oboe. *And* technique, but technique that is now a part of imagination and musicality, not something separate. Be an oboist—and a singer *and* an actor! All with expression, creativity, and imaginative technique. ➔●

To Air Is Human; To Phrase, Divine

Lynn Ann Musco

INGREDIENTS:
Clarinet students willing to listen and practice
Teachers attentive to detail

SERVES:
All clarinet players looking for more cohesive and beautiful phrasing.

Preliminary Preparation

A very common hurdle in a player's development is to overcome the lack of concept and/
or execution regarding connection, cohesion, and direction in phrasing . . . ultimately, the
art of playing musically. The ability to play with a consistent, smooth, legato style and produce a truly seamless, well-connected phrase while maintaining a well-focused and beautiful
tone is quite often not the case, and the process of how to even get to that point may elude
or frustrate even a fairly accomplished technical player. The key ingredient so often missed
between note direction and phrase cohesion, musical phrasing, and line, is all fundamen-
tally linked to the process of air. A successful, beautiful phrase is directly related to a steady,
well-paced air stream, not an air stream that the performer attempts to manipulate. I refer to
this as long-tone air—the concept of the air stream staying fully supported, never changing,
regardless of what is happening in the music . . . soft, loud, slow, fast, slurred, or articulated,
the air support is steady as if you are playing one single note. Even the youngest players can
understand the concept of long-tone air if it is introduced from the start and continuously
monitored and encouraged.

It is imperative that when attempting to embrace this concept the player understands and
executes good breathing technique. This involves not only inhaling correctly—filling the
lungs from the bottom and letting the diaphragm fully expand, but also being conscious of
how the abdominal muscles play an integral part in controlling the pace of the quantity and
speed of the air during exhalation. This can be demonstrated by the instructor by having the
student place the bell of the clarinet (or their fist, if they feel comfortable with the physical
contact—direct physical contact has a bit more demonstrational impact) mid-torso (abdominal muscles right below the rib cage and above the navel) on the instructor and push against
the instructor's body as they take a full breath. They should see the bell (or their fist) move as
the diaphragm expands (this usually causes eyes to pop and an exclamation of surprise).

Repeat this demonstration, but after inhaling play a variety of things in one breath—slow,
fast, slurred, articulated, high, low, loud, and soft, to illustrate how the abdominal muscles maintain the expanded state of the diaphragm and provide unwavering support to the

continuous column of air regardless of what type of playing you are doing. The understanding of the concept that the air does not stop is crucial to successful phrasing. It is also important that embouchure, tongue position, hand position, and finger position are addressed and monitored. The corners of the mouth should be in around the mouthpiece, the chin flat; the tongue should be high in the back of the mouth for better focus—thinking the syllable "dee" is extremely important. The hands must be comfortable and shaped in a natural curve and not cramped (right hand thumb position is significant); the fingers need to be curved, not collapsed, centered over the rings with the pinky fingers close to the auxiliary keys. Even if the air is correct, any flaws in these areas will affect the quality of the final product.

Mixing

As the conceptual ingredients of breathing, steady, directed air release, and smooth finger action are folded together, the easiest way to begin practicing and applying these concepts is through finger study exercises. Beginning players can apply these concepts to the initial exercises of any standard band method as they learn the fingerings for their very first notes—the key is to be aware and to listen to what is coming out of the end of the instrument with guidance from an attentive teacher. I like to begin with the Exercises of Mechanism (pages 16 and 17) from the Klose *Celebrated Method for Clarinet*. These are very effective for monitoring breath inhalation, paced and controlled exhalation, embouchure placement, hand position, finger placement and motion, and pitch.

It is imperative that this exercise be practiced with a metronome. Set the metronome on 60 and begin with each printed note getting one beat, do the repeat, hold the final note for an additional six or seven beats as you do a decrescendo, use one full beat to take another breath. Begin again with two notes to a beat, repeat the process, then repeat again with four notes to a beat. The entire time, the student should be concentrating on producing one steady stream of unwavering air as if he or she were playing just one note, treating every note as the first note of the interval and working for smooth, connected movement from one note to the next.

At any time the instructor can have the student hold just one note to reinforce the long-tone air concept. It is also extremely helpful for the instructor to play a steady tonic pitch as the student plays the exercise. The aural reinforcement of hearing the single steady tone will not only help the student blow a consistent, steady stream of air, but will also get them listening to the pitch of not only the unison notes but the individual intervals. It is not a priority to do the entire exercise in one breath—replenishing the air supply before the quality of sound (or pitch) suffers is crucial. The student (and instructor) will also be focusing on maintaining a well-formed embouchure (including the position of the tongue), hand position, finger motion, and listening to the evenness and consistency of sound. It is important for the instructor to monitor finger motion—no excess motion; just let the fingers move up and down.

When individually addressed the process sounds overwhelming, but with one- or two-measure exercises and attentive instruction, it is very doable and reaps wonderful results when consistently and continuously practiced with attention to detail and monitored with attentive listening from both student and teacher. Not only will the student develop strong fundamentals in regard to tone and finger technique, but they will also begin to develop and hone a sense of inner rhythm.

Baking

It is most effective to let this process bake slowly—encouraging practice of these finger studies every day with active listening skills engaged when practicing and careful attention to detail during lessons from the instructor. I encourage my students to structure their practice time much in the same way I structure their lessons, generally devoting a certain percentage of time to each area of the material being covered (i.e., one third to one half warm-up of long tones/articulation studies/scale study, one third to one half etude/literature study, depending on the level of the student and performance commitments). As the student becomes more proficient at each individual concept and technique it is up to the instructor to encourage the student to listen to the exercise as a whole—i.e., the phrase—and play through the entire phrase with no bumps, lumps, or holes, each note giving direction to the note that follows with absolutely smooth connection from note to note. Smaller portions are more appetizing and more easily digested than larger portions and yield more tasty results.

SERVING SUGGESTIONS

As the level of the player increases the finger studies can progress with the student's ability. The Klose has another section of finger studies on page 44. You can apply the same concepts to any long tone exercise (I like the expanded interval long tone studies of Russ Dagon), the Kalmen Opperman *Daily Exercises Book III*, the first two volumes of the Kroepsch *416 Progressive Studies*, and all of the Hite/Baermann *Foundation Studies Op 63* (especially the larger interval studies—fifths, sixths, sevenths, and octaves). As the concepts are solidified and honed they should be applied to every aspect of playing and to every note played; the most simple one-measure exercise, the scale played for the umpteenth time, the 30-minute concerto, all can be reduced to the smallest ingredient—moving from one note to the next, to the next, etc. It is the active listening to make sure the movement from note to note is smooth and connected with unwavering air support and constant direction that will ultimately result in a well-turned, eloquently delivered musical line. ➡

Woodwind Doubling

James Nesbit

Woodwind doubling has been an integral part of performing in all styles of music for a very long time. From an orchestral flutist doubling on piccolo, a saxophonist in a jazz ensemble doubling on clarinet, or a pit musician playing numerous instruments for a musical theater production, doubling has become a way of life for many musicians. For the professional, the most obvious advantages can be financial and making oneself marketable. For all levels of players the benefits are many and varied. Included in this are opportunities to play in musical settings reserved for what seems to always be the instruments you do not play. Sitting in a large symphony orchestra or playing in a swinging big band are equally thrilling experiences that should be enjoyed by all.

INGREDIENTS:
Woodwind players looking to enhance their overall skills and expand their musical experiences are needed for this recipe. Instruments should be in good working order.

SERVES:
All woodwind players.

In order to blur these lines and cross over to the other side requires an open mind and plenty of hard work. In addition to the obvious needs of learning another instrument or instruments there is the need to be proficient in many different styles. In many circles the term "doubler" can have some negative connotations, usually implying someone that is proficient at one instrument and plays others to a much lesser degree. I am of the firm belief that someone that is accomplished on one instrument can become equally skilled on others, but only if they apply the same work ethic and passion to the new instruments. Many musicians simply dabble rather than double because they haven't approached the instruments with the same fervor or simply consider doubling a necessary evil in the music business. Exposing students to other members of the woodwind family heightens their passion for music, gives them a deeper appreciation of widely varying styles of music, and enhances their overall musical skills.

One of the first steps in learning a new instrument starts with a concept, a mental image of the sound you are trying to create. Listening is the most effective way to accomplish this, paying close attention to every aspect of the artist's playing. Many doublers have distinct characteristics that are immediate indicators that they are playing a secondary instrument. Examples of this are the inability of reed players to taper the releases on the flute as well as their use of vibrato. The overly compact sound on the saxophone played by a clarinetist and the unfocused clarinet sound of a saxophonist are other examples. Utilizing dynamic vibrato (often referred to as diaphragm vibrato), usually reserved for flute and double reeds, on the saxophone is yet another example. Learning the nuances of an instrument is crucial for success on any instrument; it just happens to be multiplied for woodwind doublers. Sound and intonation are the hallmarks of a successful doubler; technique transfers from one instrument to another a bit easier. Always remember the only thing better than long tones are **longer tones!**

The most important part of the tone creation mechanism is where the instrument and the body meet. A correct embouchure and compatible mouthpiece/reed combination or head-joint is imperative to creating a beautiful sound. Although the clarinet and saxophone mouthpieces are very similar, they should be approached differently. Playing the clarinet stylistically correct requires a more resistant setup than the saxophone and is achieved by using a clarinet mouthpiece that has a smaller facing with a harder reed. A key thought I utilize in playing different instruments within the single reed family is the smaller the instrument, the less mouthpiece taken into the mouth.

The most common problem that occurs when reed players play the flute can be summed up in one word: placement. The position of the lip plate on the lip and the degree to which the hole is covered affects sound and intonation. It is imperative that the flute is assembled correctly, with the alignment of the head-joint on the body and the flute in the proper length. Many new flutes are made to play at A-442 and must be pulled out more than you might realize. A player can easily match the pitch on a tuning note when the flute is not in the proper length by making adjustments with the placement and position on the lip, but this will result in an inferior sound and a poor scale.

Last but not least are the double reeds, instruments I like to call the "scholarship horns." The shortage of oboe and bassoon students at the college level translates to a great deal of available scholarship money. Adding a double reed instrument to one's arsenal can open up countless playing opportunities.

Over the years I have noticed a great decline in the number of students at the college level willing to take the art of doubling seriously. The work involved in learning multiple instruments is massive but the benefits are enormous. Always remember to treat each new instrument as if it were your primary. What you learn on one will help you with the others. It is a long journey so enjoy the ride; there is a whole world of musical adventures out there waiting to be experienced.

Performance Anxiety—A Mindful Approach

Sheri Oyan

Performers of all ages suffer from some form of performance anxiety during their musical careers. The various symptoms of performance anxiety can have physical and mental manifestations, including "butterflies" in the stomach, sweaty palms, shaking, and even debilitating feelings of fear and panic. While more severe forms of performance anxiety can take months or years to conquer, less severe cases often can be dealt with effectively by practicing a few techniques taken from the study of mindfulness meditation.

INGREDIENTS:
Awareness, attention, focus, patience, practice. Mindfulness can be practiced with or without an instrument.

SERVES:
Everyone.

One of the key aspects of anxiety is that it is a fear of the unknown, i.e., "what might happen," or "what could happen," for instance. Musicians are often in the position of playing for people (teachers or peers, usually) who act as judges of musical ability. Technical mistakes while performing often lead to negative thoughts in the minds of performers—thoughts that tend to breed more negative thoughts until the performer becomes distracted and no longer focused on the music. Because of these anxiety-provoking situations, many performers are afraid to make mistakes—not just in performances, but in lessons, rehearsals, and even while practicing on their own.

The roots of mindfulness meditation come from Buddhist philosophy and religion, but the basic techniques can be practiced in a totally secular way, with no religious affiliation. The practice of building one's awareness, directing and redirecting one's attention, and noticing events in a nonjudgmental way are the fundamental keys to mindfulness. All of these fundamentals can be practiced in one's daily activities, including house cleaning, eating, walking, and playing a musical instrument.

Try this simple exercise in mindfulness while playing an instrument: Pick any note you wish, and hold the note as long as possible. While holding the note, notice all the sensations (physical and mental) that you can. For example (on a wind instrument): What do you feel in your hands/fingers? Is there tension? If so, can you release the tension? How far can you lift your fingers off of the keys before the note changes or becomes distorted? Can you feel the vibrations of the instrument? What does the instrument feel like under your fingers? Is there tension in other parts of your body? What are the sensations that occur as you run out of air? What thoughts are going through your head as you do this exercise? Are negative or distracting thoughts occurring? If you really listen, what does the note really sound like? Does the sound change as the note continues?

All of these questions are designed to get the performer to practice being really aware of all the sensations and thoughts that occur when one plays an instrument. It is amazing how little one usually notices about the sensory and mental material that accompanies the act of holding a single note. This exercise should be done on different notes, the idea being that one is simply to notice what happens. It is also important that the performer does not make any judgments about the tone quality, the sensations, etc. If one is allowed to make judgments (i.e., "This reed is terrible"), a train of thoughts will follow, taking the attention off of the task. If a distracting thought comes into the mind, one is simply to notice the thought, let it go, and redirect attention to playing the note. This exercise can be practiced in many ways—on long tones, scales, etc.

As easy as this exercise sounds, it can be difficult. One will begin to notice distracting thoughts after a certain amount of time. When this happens, just practice redirecting the attention, again without judgment (i.e., refrain from thinking, "I'm not good at this," "This is pointless," etc.).

Daily mindfulness practice can help the performer become less distracted by anxious thoughts, physical sensations, etc. and become more focused on the music. Musicians often feel helpless against the thoughts and/or physical sensations brought on by performance anxiety because they allow themselves to be "carried away" by thoughts and feelings. Refining the skills of noticing, letting go, and redirecting attention can help prepare musicians deal with distractions and anxiety during performance. Practicing mindfulness in various situations everyday will eventually carry over into practicing mindfulness during potentially stressful performances.

Leftover Ingredients
The skills developed in mindfulness practice can also be used to combat physical problems and technical problems while playing, including muscular tension, lip-biting (reed instruments), uneven finger movement, etc. Playing slowly while noticing physical sensations can bring some of these problems into awareness, making the problems easier to fix. For example, students often do not realize or believe they are "biting" into the reed. By playing an ascending scale slowly and mindfully, the student will eventually feel the biting occur with each ascending pitch, and will be more likely to work to stop the biting. ➡

Working as a Woodwind Doubler

Elsie Parker

Warning! This can be very time consuming!

INGREDIENTS:
Good equipment, patience

SERVES:
A woodwind player interested in a rewarding, interesting, fun, challenging, and ever-changing way of making a living doing what *you* want.

Good Equipment
Buy the best instruments that you can afford. Keep your instruments in good playing condition. As a woodwind doubler, I prefer using rather "easy blowing" setups, especially on the instruments beyond clarinet, my main instrument. For me, it is important to find mouthpieces and reeds that work easily for my instruments. There simply is not enough time in a day to work on that many reeds . . . Buy the best reeds and mouthpieces you can get your hands on. These involve a lot of experimentation, trying new things, new products, and is a never-ending search.

If you are playing in your own pop/jazz group (or also work as a vocalist, which I do), you might also want to buy the best easy-to-pack *sound* equipment you can afford. If, like me, you did not originally know *anything* at all about sound equipment, get advice from people who *do* have experience with and regularly use microphones, mixers, speakers, etc. in their line of work. There is a lot of technology that can help you. MiniDisc recorders and iPods were big revelations to me!

Patience
You'll need lots and lots of patience in practicing *almost* everyday. Have patience during the times when you are less busy with work, utilize your "down time" to prepare by practicing your doubles, work on reeds, write music, make contacts for work.

Listen, Read, Improvise
Listen to music of *many* types: classical, jazz, popular, vocal music, and music for instruments *other* than your own. Read music in *many* styles . . . classical music, show music, written-out jazz . . . learn to improvise. Sight reading skills are **very** important when you are doing show work, and often get very little rehearsal time. Starting as a strictly classically trained clarinetist, I really had some catching up to do on learning to read pop/jazz/swing rhythms to play shows and play in big bands.

Books that can help your jazz style reading tremendously on *any* woodwind instrument are saxophone books by Lennie Niehaus (*Jazz Conception*, basic through advanced), Joe Viola, (*Studies, Vol. 3*, the duets) and Joe Allard (*Advanced Rhythms* . . . these are killer!). Play written-out jazz transcriptions of famous player's solos *and* transcribe them for yourself. Learn to play something *wonderful* from *memory* on all your instruments. Play along with CDs. Learn to play as many instruments as you can handle. Practice them *regularly*. Don't just be a "reed *owner*" . . .

Pleasantness

Be pleasant on jobs and at rehearsals. Be positive in your contact with fellow musicians. Be cooperative with conductors. Embrace the role you are musically playing, whether it is first or last chair . . . Don't get a reputation for canceling for better work or you will soon have no work.

R & R

Give yourself a break when you need it. Treat yourself to a vacation occasionally. Getting some exercise every day keeps you in good physical and mental shape and prevents stress from accumulating. (I *make the time* to swim laps for one half hour almost *every day*.) Eat healthily.

Heroes

Meet *in person* great performers whose music you admire. *Go ahead* . . . go hear/see them, get to know them whenever possible. Develop some heroes, people about whose music you feel **passionate**. *See* how they act, perform on stage. The *self confidence* that some performers convey can be a whole lesson in itself.

Promotion

Unless you have an agent representing you, you will need to be promoting yourself. Make business cards. Develop a logo and/or a name of a group that people begin to recognize. Do phone interviews, radio interviews, TV shows when invited. Learn to operate your own Web site and keep it up to date. Read the arts & entertainment calendars. Read the arts sections of newspapers and magazines to learn about possible places to contact. Look at the phone book. There you will find listings for museums, restaurants, concert series, concert venues, country clubs, and art galleries. Try to make some kind of contact *almost every day* concerning work. Send e-mails to people who have hired you in the past to let them know where you are performing. Remind them that you exist, and the *different* kinds of music you can perform. Work with the best musicians you can. Play duets with that are better than you are!

Join your local musician's union! Most professional orchestral and theater work requires that you belong to your local union. Use the union directory to get to know other professional musicians and contractors. Get to know the contractors for theater orchestras in your area. Audition for these orchestras, or to be on an extra player list. Start paying into your local musician's union pension plan.

Diversity

Learn to play your "main" instrument as well as you possibly can. If you are short on time, make sure you play your "main" instrument . . . but learn to play the others and spend as much time as you possibly can on them. A goal might be to play your doubles so well that your audience and fellow musicians are *not be able to tell* which your "main" instrument is.

Learn to do other kinds of music other than what you originally intended to . . . If you're an instrumentalist, you might learn to sing. If you think that, as an instrumentalist, you are not wonderful at singing, remember that the many instrumentalists who added singing to their vocabulary—trumpet player Chet Baker, trumpet player Louis Armstrong, saxophone player James Moody, drummer Mel Torme—people *loved* it when they sang . . . *as much or more* than when they were playing their instruments! Or, take *my* personal favorite . . . Argentinian tenor saxophonist Gato Barbieri. He's not exactly *singing*, . . . more *chanting* some exotic poetry . . . When he adds that very sensual *"Hey!"* or *"Ohh . . . "* to his already wonderful instrumental playing, the effect is priceless.

In addition to being a woodwind doubler on clarinet, E-flat clarinet, bass clarinet, flute, piccolo, alto flute, soprano sax, alto sax, and tenor sax, I also sing French popular music *in French* . . . songs of Edith Piaf, Charles Aznavour, Michel Legrand, Vanessa Paradis (Johnny Depp's girlfriend). I've recorded three CDs of French songs, have my own very active group, have had orchestrations written for me, and have performed numerous times with symphony orchestras as a *vocal* soloist. Learning to sing in a popular style *can* be done *on your own* . . . you don't *have* to go back to school for a degree in this. It's purely fun and enjoyable for me, and often generates as large a part of my income as does woodwind doubling. ➤

Bassoon Reed Taste Test: A Recipe for the Best Intonation and Response

Richard Polonchak

Many band/orchestra directors and bassoon students do not know that every bassoon reed has a "good side" and a "bad side." The good side will always face the sky or ceiling and the bad side will always face the floor or the ground. Professionals spend time play-testing reeds so that they can determine which side will go on top. The so-called "good side" is actually the side that has a little less cane (wood) on it—it is the lighter side. The so-called "bad side" is the side that has slightly more cane on it—the heavier side. It is humanly impossible to get both sides of the reed exactly alike—even the most skilled reedmaker will never be able to get both sides totally equal. Because the bassoon embouchure is an "overbite" with a slight pressure from the bottom jaw, the reed's heavier side goes against this bottom jaw. The lower jaw/lip pushes *slightly* against the heavier reed side and makes it "think" that it is equal to the lighter side. Then the whole system is balanced and the bassoon will have the best intonation and easy response.

INGREDIENTS:
A bassoon in good repair with a good bocal and a bassoon reed that blows freely, supports the middle register, and is able to play throughout the entire dynamic range from very soft to very loud

SERVES:
All bassoon players and all ensembles that include bassoons.

Like a master chef will taste test the final creation and make adjustments based on how a recipe feels to the palate, the bassoonist must "taste test" the reed to choose the side that offers the best intonation and response. Below is a series of tests that I personally use to determine which side of the reed goes on top. When my reeds pass all the tests successfully, I put a small pencil mark on that side of the reed (like an "x" or a "0")—then that side will be played on top.

Taste Test Number 1
On the "wrong side of the reed", these notes will be very flat or won't speak at all.

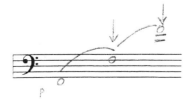

Play the low F softly and then slur to the open F. Just let the second F come out without any embouchure adjustment. On the correct side of the reed, the open F will not be flat. Then, slur to the high F (still playing softly). The correct side of the reed will produce the most in-tune high F. *The side with the least amount of bottom lip/jaw pressure to put the note in tune will be the correct side.*

Taste Test Number 2
On the "wrong" side of the reed, this note will be very flat or won't speak at all.

Play the C as softly as possible and then slur to E. The correct side of the reed will give the most in-tune E.

Taste Test Number 3
On the wrong side of the reed, the upper D will be flat.

On the wrong side, the Fs will be very flat or won't speak at all.

Play these eighth notes very softly and do not "push" to get the slurs. Notice which side produces the F easily and in tune. Listen for flat high notes—choose the side that produces good response and intonation.

Taste Test Number 4

Courante from the third Bach Cello Suite No. 3

Playing as softly as possible, listen for the best response on the Fs and E-flats. For this test, play the E-flats using only first and third fingers of the left hand plus the whisper key. Do not use any extra fingers/keys in the right hand to help with intonation.

Taste Test Number 5
Listen for which side these notes sound flat (play very softly).

Playing as softly as possible, listen for the side of the reed that lets the higher notes both speak and speak in tune.

Taste Test Number 6

Test to see which side of the reed produces the most in-tune and present upper D. Do not make embouchure adjustments for the test—let the correct side of the reed be the support here.

Taste Test Number 7

First Haydn, London Trio, second movement

Play the eighth notes as softly as you can. See which side of the reed allows the last note to speak without any "push" from breath—the correct side of the reed will allow the final G to speak in the diminuendo at the end of the phrase.

Taste Test Number 8

Beethoven, Violin Concerto, second movement

Play this as softly as possible. Using no embouchure adjustment, see which side of the reed produces the best High F#. It may not even speak using the bad side of the reed.

Taste Test Number 9

Tschaikowsky, Symphony No. 4

One side of the reed will produce the very best intonation with the least amount of adjustment from the player's embouchure.

On a final note, remember to play softly as the tests are being performed—and also to not do big embouchure adjustments for tuning purposes. Playing softly and not adjusting with the embouchure will force the reed to "do the work." And one side of the reed will do a better job of doing that work than the other.

I put the reed through these tests and also add others—including any current solo passages that I might have in the various ensembles that I'm part of. It's amazing what a difference it makes if I'm not playing on the correct side of the reed. Of course, some reeds are more balanced from top side to bottom side than others. The closer the balance, the more difficult it becomes to choose which side of the reed is best. Inadvertently, in testing out the reed, the bassoonist may make "automatic" embouchure adjustments to both sides of the reed. That is the reason I like to put the reed through several tests. For me, it helps keep the testing more objective and keeps giving me a "reference frame" from which to look and hear. And if you hear your bassoonist having difficulty with response or intonation (or both) with a solo passage in a band or orchestra rehearsal, you might say, "Try turning the reed over and play that passage on the other side." That may be all it takes! ➞●

Orchestral Performance: Preparing for the First Rehearsal

Richard Ramey

How do you prepare an orchestral piece for performance? Do you feel confident in every rehearsal or does your mind work against you, causing needless slip-ups? Try the following recipe for rehearsal preparation and see if you don't feel better about your performances both in a rehearsal setting and on the stage!

INGREDIENTS:
Instrument, orchestra part, recording, composer biography, music history text

SERVES:
All musicians when applied with diligence.

Defining the problem:
From the first lesson we are all taught techniques for learning new compositions. These mostly involve learning ways to play difficult passages while playing the work in a stylistically appropriate manner. Although this is a good start, orchestra preparation is a multifaceted task that goes much deeper. Unlike school or community orchestras, which may spend weeks preparing for one concert, the professional orchestra does not have the luxury of an abundance of rehearsals. Professional players must do their prerehearsal preparation and keep in mind: *Ensemble* is the sole reason why orchestra rehearsals exist.

Being adequately prepared on a new work will allow you to attend rehearsals feeling confident of the part and of your playing . . . elements crucial for a successful performance. Your goal is to keep mistakes at an absolute minimum, which will, in turn, establish your reputation. Good or bad, your reputation will spread throughout the musical community. The underlying concept of adequate preparation:

Think of every rehearsal as a performance.

Preparation techniques:
Try to obtain the music as far in advance as possible by consulting the season brochure and the orchestra librarian. For non-rental works, consider purchasing not only your part but the entire section's parts. You may play this work many times in your life and you can be assured of having your part early. You will also have a part that is now marked with valuable cues, thus saving you preparation time in future performances. Frequently, audition committees ask for tutti sections, not just the usual exposed solo passages and having complete parts will allow you to prepare adequately. Most standard orchestral works are published by a handful

of large companies such as Kalmus and Luck's, and can be accessed online. If you don't know the specific publisher of the work, contact a sheet music distributor who can locate the publisher via their reference books. Orchestral parts are now being sold as composer collections on CD-ROM.

You should obtain a recording of the piece . . . many are readily available at university music libraries, community libraries, or from a teacher or colleague. Many university libraries now have online audio recording databases such as Naxos and Classical Music Library, so you may listen to the work directly on your computer. Scores of standard orchestral works are available in inexpensive editions and would be a valuable tool in your preparation.

Once you have the recording, listen to it with a definite plan in mind. Your first step is to listen to the work in its entirety without stopping to mark cues in your music. On the second time through, listen with the intent of writing cues and tempi in the music by starting and stopping the recording frequently. Listening more than once will allow you to have a better understanding of the work as a whole and how individual lines come together to create that whole. Even if you've performed the work in the past, refreshing your memory will give you that much-needed confidence in the performance. If you have never performed the work, studying it via recordings will give you a feeling of having performed it several times as you become intimately aware of the work's various components. I am constantly amazed at how many musicians don't listen to a work because they "don't have time," when in fact listening *saves time and is an integral part of the preparation.* Developing a habit of listening, practicing, and researching numerous pieces at the same time will allow the performer to really get into a groove that ultimately becomes a lot of fun and beats "just practicing." The *variety* in a preparation sequence makes the outcome more effective. As times goes by, one becomes more and more efficient with all of these steps.

An orchestral musician should take the time to conduct basic research into the background of the composer and the composition. Search for information online; check standard reference sources such as *The New Grove Dictionary of Music and Musicians.* Consult composers' biographies, which are often found at your local library. To make your research more succinct, keep in mind that you are only looking for a brief background concerning the composer's personal life, compositional style, and facts that surround the compositional period in which the work was written. By gaining insight into the stylistic interpretation of the piece, your performance will be greatly enhanced!

Learn the notes (completely!) *before* the first rehearsal. Take the time to learn technical spots slowly, so you can eventually play them cleanly at tempo. A useful technique is to set a metronome on subdivided beats; this helps in feeling the inner pulse of the passage. In practice sessions, do not play mistakes or play uncleanly. This in essence allows your mind to reinforce these problems. When practicing parts of a technical passage remember the *Rule of Ten*: with your metronome set at a very slow tempo, play the small part ten times in a row—perfectly—before increasing the speed slightly. If you make a mistake during that time, go back to number one and start again. What seems to be a lengthy procedure actually ends up saving time because you are learning the passage correctly and avoid the need to "fix" things later.

Don't make the mistake of avoiding the practice of slow, lyrical lines or even entire movements just because they appear to be easy and you are facing time constraints. One of the most difficult concepts to learn is the art of playing musically by shaping and molding a phrase; like everything else, this mastery takes *practice.* As musicians, we are always focused on the technical aspects of a composition—that is, in "getting the notes." As you practice these slower sections, make sure that your attacks are gentle, are at the correct dynamic, and above all, in tune. For wind players, it is important to make sure that the note ending a phrase is tapered to nothing, rather than abruptly cut off. Think of how a string player ends a note and the lingering sound that occurs after the bow stops. Always try to imitate this effect on your wind instrument. As you play through these melodies, *listen* to what you hear. Ask yourself: "Is this good?" "What is the melody trying to say and am I conveying that message?" Sing the melody and then try to duplicate it on your instrument. As a bassoonist, I find this one technique to be invaluable in learning to play a melody with style and grace.

A recording is useful not only in learning the work aurally, but doing run-through performances by playing with it in practice sessions. Playing with the recording is actually like having an additional rehearsal with the orchestra! This technique will give you a feel for subtle tempo changes, a better idea of how your part fits in with certain orchestral sections, and with the work as a whole. Resist becoming too accustomed to the recording. Even though standard orchestral works are usually performed in time-tested ways, each conductor will have his or her own interpretation and you should mark your part accordingly. As you near the date of the first rehearsal, you'll probably feel as though you know the work. Don't slack off; do keep practicing! You won't need a lot of intense work, IF you have done your homework. You will, however, need to keep the piece within your fingers. Do this at your practice session by quickly reviewing a few technical spots, then perform an entire movement (including the whole notes and rests!) without stopping. Doing this twice a week will give you the sense of having "performed" the work several times by the actual date of the concert.

Be generous with accidentals written in the part. Place these in locations where there is ANY tendency to play a wrong note. Professional players' lives tend to be quite hectic so it behooves us to prepare the part so that it can be played perfectly under any extenuating circumstances. This technique of marking has saved me countless times in rehearsals and performances. Also remember to translate all unfamiliar tempo indications in the music (especially important for nineteenth-century German works).

Here is a list of music cues that I use:

- Upward or downward arrows over noteheads to indicate pitch corrections . . . this would include chord voicing.
- If needed, write in trill fingerings so that you can decipher in a glance.
- For long, extended passages, or for passages written for an orchestral section (such as the woodwinds) where all must play in synch, write in breath cues; if breathing is a problem in long passages indicate this, too.
- In patterned music with rests (think a long series of off-beats), where the pattern momentarily changes, circle this change so that you don't come in during the rest.
- For unclear rhythm passages place vertical lines above the staff to indicate beats.
- Indicate deviations in the meter ("in four," "in eight," "sub four").
- To indicate quick ritards or accelerandos, place horizontal arrows in the part.
- In passages where accents appear in unconventional places, circle the accents.
- In passages where *sf* appears, place a marcato mark (inverted "V") over the note to quickly distinguish this note from a regular note.
- During long rests, be generous with instrumental cues (that is, indicate which instrument is entering at any given section).
- Word cues that indicate who you are linked with in a passage are very helpful: "w/cl," w/2nd," "w/vlns," "w/brass," "tutti," "solo," "soli," "ww's," "join clar."

- In passages where your part is a continuous series of repeated notes (such as a long series of eighths) of both accompaniment and then melody, place phrase markings in the music that indicate where the accompaniment stops and the melody begins.
- Mark in mechanical cues such as indications to watch the conductor or a section of the orchestra whose part lines up with yours. Mark technical considerations unique to your instrument (as with bassoon: "lok on," or "lok off").
- If applicable, remind yourself of the current clef after a long series of rests.
- Make repeat signs stand out and actually draw arrows leading back to the start of the repeat (especially helpful in music with many repeats such as a Strauss waltz or a minuet/trio movement of a symphony).
- Mark in prominent instrumental cues right before you enter; an example might be a pickup note in one solo instrument that plays right before enter.
- Standard word cues include: *time*, appearing at the end of a page, letting you know that you don't need to quickly turn the page and play; *V.S.*, or "volti subito" ("turn quickly"); my own word cue, *V.S.S.*, or "turn the page really quickly!", when the part give you no time to turn the page; *attaca*, indicating that the next movement begins immediately; *segue* indicating that the next movement continues immediately, with no loss of time; *tune*, to indicate your part is now the melody (in places where this wouldn't normally be recognized); *no-vib* to indicate non-vibrato, *under oboe*, to indicate that your part must remain as a support for the prominent instrument; *count*, usually appearing in a long series of rests where your next entrance is crucial.
- In a mostly scalar line where one larger skip appears, indicate this skip by placing an inverted "V" above it (this reminds you that the passage is not totally scalar).

The date of the first rehearsal has arrived. Be at the rehearsal location, set up and ready to play, at least 30 minutes prior to the downbeat. This allows plenty of time to find the hall, assemble your instrument and accessories, warm up, and if applicable, to test reeds. Remember: *think of every rehearsal as a performance*. It is hoped that by following these suggestions the player will have confidence in himself and perform as flawlessly as possible. Know *what to expect; don't be surprised by anything in the music*. There are two occasions when people form opinions about your playing: at the first rehearsal and at the performance. Make sure that you are ready for both. ➤●

Why Etudes? A Guide for Woodwind Players and Doublers

Albert Regni

INGREDIENTS:
Etudes

SERVES:
Woodwind players and doublers.

As a student, I remember asking, why I was knocking myself out practicing a Rosé etude on the clarinet or a Ferling oboe transcription (of all things!) on the saxophone or a Karg-Elert etude on the flute? What good was this doing and wouldn't it be more beneficial to be learning an orchestral etude or digging into the Mozart clarinet concerto or memorizing the Ibert *Concertino Da Camera* or "perfecting" the Poulenc flute sonata, or working on a saxophone/clarinet/flute orchestral etude or even running through "rhythm" changes? (Talk about being scatterbrained.) We all know that there is so much that we *have* to know, what will an etude do for us? We only have so much time, so why not put it to use working on something that is a more obvious requirement for a "real" performance? (You know the old saying, "So much music; so little time.")

A short while into my professional career I began to realize the importance of a constant regimen of disciplined preparation and performance of unfamiliar etudes. The preparation of a new etude for each of my weekly lesson sessions provided that outlet. (Yes, I did continue to take weekly lessons well into my professional career.) The benefits of constantly planning and "working out" of (new) materials have a far-reaching carryover effect that not only contributes to one's technical mastery of an instrument, but also to the musicality of the individual involved. It is also quite important to realize that "doubling" requires a great deal of organization and continuous prudent preparation. Proficiency on any instrument requires the performer to have the technical and physical competency necessary to play through a piece in its entirety without interruption.

From the most elementary to the most advanced, new etudes require a discipline that is unique and very important to a musician's development, instrumentally and otherwise. Having to work out new musical problems on a consistent basis within the form of an etude, or even a short musical vignette, is an important part of regular practice. Let's look at some of the considerations and the benefits to be derived from following through on them.

Before we attempt to play a note, a primary requisite in the planning of an etude is to consider the tonalities and mood of the work and to what significance are these in relation to

113

the overall piece. A couple of questions we can ask ourselves at the outset are: "Is this a major key with a spirited mood or a serene etude, in a minor key, with a lyrical approach needed?" I often ask students to aurally "visualize" how they would sing the work in preparation, before they attempt at playing it. Thinking about how the music should come together and having a concept of the piece in your "mind's ear" aids in the focus necessary for a good finished product. At times our tendency as instrumentalists is to give more attention to the instrument than to the music we are playing.

Editing an etude is tantamount to good performance. Knowing and marking the breaths not only gives the music and performer the necessary pacing, but also helps to define the intent of the music. The effects of pauses and silences between phrases create a dramatic sense of tension and release for the listener. As in poetry or speechmaking, a sense of timing is very important to delivering an effective message. We have heard many times that music is a universal language, but as in communicating in any tongue, music must be defined not only by its content but by its delivery as well. Knowing in advance *where to breathe* should be considered a primary step in our preparation process.

Playing a phrase requires a feeling and understanding of a musical line. This is where the "artistic" qualities began to emerge. Dynamics are certainly in consideration here but relating the markings to an actual sound requires sensitivity to good basic musical principles. We need to play softly but not too softly. How much crescendo is needed? These are only a couple of the questions we need to consider in our quest for the definitive performance of our chosen work. How an individual phrase should be presented in terms of dynamic nuance needs to be considered so as not to be overplayed or visa versa. Good lyrical connection of succeeding notes is an ever-present matter to be dealt with, remembering that our ultimate goal is to present music that will be satisfying and interesting to our listener(s).

Technical etudes **require slow, methodical preparation** so that the benefit of even and flawless lines and articulations are attained. Lyrical melodic pieces require breath control, vibrato consistency, and attention to intervallic balance. Many considerations must go into our personal masterpiece. As we begin to consider these parts, the realization of what one must work for in attaining a quality performance takes shape and spurs us on. When the pieces are put together in a prudent manner, the player's readiness to perform is suddenly enhanced and the desire to perform is not so boggled by "performance anxiety." In fact, when preparation is beyond adequate, we yearn to perform and are "chomping at the bit" for the listener's ear.

After preparing an etude sufficiently, we many times realize that much of what we considered to be music fit only for the practice room works very well before an audience. Solo performance of etudes not only gives the listener the benefit of the presenter's technical and artistic abilities, but a glance at the personal musical characteristics of the performer as well.

Everyone has his or her own thumbprint when it comes to performance, as in any art form, and etude presentations are wonderful methods of showing off individuality, virtuosity, and musicality.

Since etudes are not always heard outside of the practice room, or mostly for your teacher's ears only, we must not lose sight of Ralph Waldo Emerson's wonderful words of wisdom: "The reward from doing something well is to have done it." I would carry this a step further and add that the reward of consistent etude preparation enhances one's instrumental performance security. ➤

Successful Pie Dough and Rich, FlavorFul-filling

Ibby Roberts

A recipe that can be used by students to create success and fulfillment throughout their lives, with some morsels for professionals, too!

INGREDIENTS:
Creativity
Consistent daily routine
Honest self-evaluation
High standards
Great education
Teachability
Professionalism and business-mindedness
Healthy living

SERVES:
People who care.

The dough is the foundation. Be creative as you imagine the shape into which you will knead your dough, and know that you can change its form as you work with it.

Have a challenging daily routine and modify it to meet your needs. Select exercises that keep your fingers and embouchure in shape, and that continuously improve your technique. These should be a combination of scales and arpeggios, long tones, etudes, and specific techniques, such as double tonguing and vibrato, or intonation work. Do these every day along with working on any repertoire you need to prepare at a given time.

Ask yourself what your strengths and weaknesses are as a player, and be honest in this process. Don't be overly critical, and don't ignore things that need attention. Certain abilities come more naturally to each of us, while other skills take more work. Maximize your strengths and fix your weaknesses so that you are a well-rounded player and are not held back by your technique in any area. Similarly, work through your personal hang-ups so that you can fulfill your potential as an artist. Challenge yourself and be determined to succeed. Remember that art begins where technique leaves off.

Hold yourself to the highest standards—if something is not good, work hard to improve it. Don't settle by telling yourself that it will do as is, and don't allow yourself to make excuses. Just go for it; do the work that it takes to play well. Have clear goals, both near and long range, for these will provide direction for you in your study and preparation. Be aware of what you are working towards, and be clear on how you will get there. Own the highest quality

115

instrument you can afford (it's worth stretching here) and keep it in great repair so you are not held back by your equipment. And if you play a reed instrument, make lots and lots of reeds so that you always have a good one in your box to use, no matter when duty calls.

Pick a great teacher, whether you are in middle school, high school, college, or conservatory. Find a teacher who has a good personality match with you; who loves what he/she does; who can provide you with the tools necessary to play your instrument well; who is articulate and can explain to you how to do things on your instrument—the insiders' tricks of the trade; and whose name will open doors for your down the road. (During my training, my three main teachers, Arthur Weisberg, Stephen Maxym, and Richard Polonchak, offered much wisdom and life-changing instruction. Throughout my professional career, I have added my own flavor to the mix they provided, making their ideas my own and passing them along my students.)

Similarly, pick a great school, one that has a curriculum that offers you the knowledge and experience that will properly train you in your field. Get the necessary formal training to reach your goals—how we look on paper nowadays impacts the opportunities that lie in front of us.

Be open to suggestion by your teachers and your peers. No one has all of the answers, so be ready to be challenged. Try new techniques and approaches. Once you have wholeheartedly tried them, then you can evaluate if they work for you or not. Be a problem solver—again, don't settle knowing that something is difficult; set your goal and find a solution to the problem. Don't cover it up or hide it! Ask for evaluation by other respected colleagues and teachers, not just people who play or teach your primary instrument. Take risks—trust your instincts and throw a little something extra into the pie on occasion; the new flavors will make you stretch and will surprise you in good ways.

Create opportunities for yourself and make connections with colleagues and teachers. Be supportive and be a team player. Join and form performing groups, from youth orchestras to chamber ensembles; and go to music camps and festivals to get experience beyond what you obtain in school, places where you can focus completely on performing and perfecting your abilities on your instrument. Take preprofessional-level work in order to obtain experience when you are young. Jump at opportunities. Act professionally at all times. How you show up makes a huge difference in whether or not the phone rings again and whether or not your name is passed along to other contractors and personnel managers.

As wind players, just like for singers, how we treat our bodies impacts how well we can do our jobs. Take care of your body—exercise, eat healthy foods, and get proper rest. Activities like yoga that increase your body awareness can also impact your playing in a positive way. The better you care for your body, the more energy you'll have for making great music. Find an approach that feels natural to you. Be well rounded as a person—do more than play your instrument. Participate in activities that are unrelated to music; get to know people; live life. All of this will benefit your interpretation of the music.

Rich, FlavorFul-filling Ingredients:

> Be True to Yourself.
> Express Creatively.
> Give One Hundred Percent.

There is great pressure to be "number one" in our society, but there are so many talented people in each field that we cannot all be number one, despite the fact that many might deserve this honor. Many artists find it difficult to feel fulfilled by the success in their lives when compared with this unrealistic standard. Similarly it can be difficult for young students to be realistic about the opportunities that lie ahead of them, unaware of what it takes to be successful in those opportunities, and perhaps even unaware of the opportunities altogether. There are many more qualified players than there are positions in major orchestras; and even less opportunities exist for musicians seeking solo careers. Therefore many talented artists need to create professional lives filled with a variety of musical activities, blending teaching and performing, and frequently requiring a non-music-related job in order to be financially secure. This type of life can still be successful and fulfilling, even if it doesn't meet society's standard of being "number one."

It is possible to be a great and expressive artist without having fame. Fulfillment can come throughout life in many forms. It is important for each young artist to define for him/herself what success means; and it is the responsibility of teachers to help their students figure out what role they want music to play in their lives, and to help them achieve their goals.

Live your life in a way that allows you to have time and space to be imaginative and express yourself creatively. There are certainly standards to uphold and accepted ways of interpreting different works and styles, but look for what you see in the music. Don't simply copy what you've been told to do or what you've heard on recordings. Use these sources as a guide, but find your own voice and put your ideas into your own words. The more you know yourself, the freer you'll be as a person, and the better you'll be at expressing yourself through the music, which in turn will provide the greatest fulfillment.

In closing, the more you put into life, the more you will get out of it. We hear that expression frequently, but it is worth it, because it is true. ➝●

How Should I Test a Saxophone Mouthpiece?

Eugene Rousseau

INGREDIENTS:
Several good reeds
Your favorite old mouthpiece and one or more new ones
Your instrument, in good working condition

SERVES:
Anyone who cares deeply about his/her sound and intonation.

The question or how to test a saxophone mouthpiece is a good one and deserves a straightforward answer. Five steps should be taken in testing a mouthpiece:

1. Use several reeds of slightly different strengths. Your favorite reed is probably comfortable on your current mouthpiece.
2. Be certain that the reed is placed correctly on the mouthpiece, that its tip is even with the mouthpiece tip, and that it is centered from side to side.
3. Does the reed seal? Keeping the end covered, draw the air out of it and then take the mouthpiece from your mouth. A popping sound means that the reed is fitting properly on the mouthpiece. A warped reed will not pop because air is escaping between it and the mouthpiece.

4. Tune third-line B on alto, tenor, or baritone saxophone, or top-line F-sharp on soprano to its respective concert pitch. This note may be tuned slightly flat but never sharp. Improper mouthpiece position can cause bad intonation, poor response, and inferior tone quality.

5. Do some playing in all registers, from lyrical to rapid staccato, using various dynamic levels. Repeat the examples several times, and then play them, using your own reed and mouthpiece. Now try the new mouthpiece and reed again. May players like to record this test, which allows them to "stand back and listen." Some prefer to have one or more musician-friends listen as each mouthpiece is played. If you use these "judges," be sure that they cannot see which mouthpiece is being played. Listen with your ears, not with your eyes. Be patient. Mouthpiece testing takes time. Finally, how does the new mouthpiece feel to you? To make the right decision you must like the way it feels.

Good luck.

Defining the Parts of the Saxophone Mouthpiece

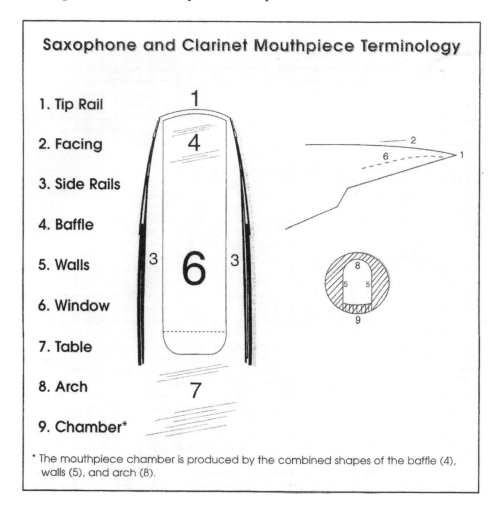

Saxophone and Clarinet Mouthpiece Terminology

1. Tip Rail
2. Facing
3. Side Rails
4. Baffle
5. Walls
6. Window
7. Table
8. Arch
9. Chamber*

* The mouthpiece chamber is produced by the combined shapes of the baffle (4), walls (5), and arch (8).

The tip rail contributes to the brightness or darkness of a tone; a thinner, narrower tip allows for higher partials—thus more brightness. The facing is actually comprised of two curves—two side rails—one on each side of the mouthpiece, so it is important that these are symmetrical. Each brand of mouthpiece has a number or letter that designates the facing, referring primarily to the tip opening, i.e., the distance between the reed and the mouthpiece at the very tip. A larger number indicates a greater opening, but the designations do not usually indicate the length of the facing. The baffle is the area inside the mouthpiece that is directly underneath the reed. The distance from the reed to the baffle is critical in determining brightness and darkness of the tone. Generally, a higher baffle, i.e., closer to the reed, produces a brighter tone. The walls normally come straight down from the top of the side rails to the baffle.

Early examples of the saxophone mouthpiece were often concave, while some jazz mouthpieces (E. Rousseau JMA and JMT) have the walls descending diagonally from the side rails. The window is the opening between the side rails that is covered by the reed. The reed rests on the table to provide a good seal between reed and mouthpiece; the table must be kept clean and smooth. E. Rousseau hard rubber mouthpieces are designed to have a very slight concave area in the center of the table to ensure a secure fit for the reed. The arch is located between the table at the end of the window, and can be easily seen by looking through the mouthpiece form round end to tip. The chamber is a combination of the shapes of the baffle, walls, and arch. ➤●

High-Altitude Performing

Rebecca Kemper Scarnati

Playing and singing at high altitudes require special approaches to preparation and performing. Simply put, the higher the altitude, the less atmosphere present. We will define high altitude as levels four thousand feet and above, although one may sense differences at any change in altitude. For most people, being at high altitude simply means using a lot of sunscreen or making adjustments in cooking times. For those of us performing at high altitudes, we notice less oxygen, drier atmosphere, less air available to move, and—for reed players—nonvibrating, closed reeds.

INGREDIENTS:

Water, as much as you can stand to drink.
Good breathing techniques.
Extra breath marks in the music.
Patience—you cannot do at altitude what you do at sea level.
48 hours at altitude whenever possible before a performance.
Healthy heart. If you are under a doctor's care for heart problems you might want to consult with him/her before going to higher altitudes.
Reed players: longer reeds made from smaller diameter cane.

SERVES:

Anyone traveling to altitudes above four thousand feet (which covers most of the inland Western United States). But this is especially for those using wind and, even more especially, for those who use reeds (with special emphasis on oboe reeds).

PREPARATION:

Water: High altitudes are drier places because there is less atmosphere. You cannot wait until you are thirsty to start drinking because at that point you are already dehydrated. Athletes start drinking more water about forty-eight hours before an event, as do successful hikers of the Grand Canyon. At high altitudes, musicians need to do the same thing. Two days before you go to a higher altitude start drinking more water, but especially two days before a performance. Those who attempt the Canyon without drinking water in advance often have to be taken out by emergency helicopter. It is amazing how quickly people dehydrate at altitude without realizing it.

Those of us who have lived in the clouds for a long time often keep water bottles with us continually and make sure that we drink several bottles per day. Dehydration causes almost flu-like symptoms. Also keep in mind that I mean water: not tea, coffee, or any other drink with caffeine. Caffeine dries you out. I am not saying that you cannot have a cup of coffee in the morning, but follow it up with a big glass of water. When performing, be sure to keep a bottle of water beside you and drink often.

Reed players, you need to constantly wet your reeds. If you have a long passage of several minutes without several measures rest, you may need to plan to wet the reed as you take a breath. I have had to do this when playing concertos with bands and orchestras in Flagstaff, Arizona. The first time that I played a concerto at seven thousand feet, I got near the end of a long passage and the reed almost stopped playing because it had actually dried out as I was playing!

Good breathing techniques are essential at high altitude. There is less oxygen available, so you will need to take more frequent and deeper breaths. The good news is that the air that is available at seven thousand feet is cleaner than in lower-altitude cities. Two of the cities cited as having the cleanest air in the US are Colorado Springs, Colorado and Flagstaff, Arizona—both at seven thousand feet. Those with breathing problems, like asthma, generally do not have problems with less air at higher altitudes. You will need to take more breaths at higher altitudes especially if you are performing less than forty-eight hours after arriving (see the forty-eight-hour recommendation below). If you have any trouble or come close to running out of air at sea level in a phrase of music, plan on taking an extra breath at high altitude. Don't even try to go without the extra breath; you won't make it.

Wind players may also find low-note response and fast articulation a bit more difficult because there is less air to move. This is where excellent breathing techniques are essential. You have to have a lot of air pressure behind articulations and low notes. I tell my students that if you can do it at seven thousand feet you can do it anywhere. In Flagstaff, Arizona where I live, we are designated a high-altitude Olympic training city and athletes from all over the world come here to train. Perhaps musicians should take a cue from athletes and come to higher altitudes to learn to breathe.

Forty-eight hours adjustment time to higher altitudes is highly recommended. It takes forty-eight hours for the hemoglobin in the human body to adjust to oxygen level changes that occur when you change altitudes. For those of us who live at higher altitudes and then descend to sea level, this means we have at least forty-eight hours when we feel like super men and women! But for those coming to high altitude, this means that you will find yourself out of breath and may suffer from an altitude headache. If you work out, you will have to lighten it up especially during the first forty-eight hours. When playing, this means that you will run out of air and tire more quickly. I am often told by visitors that they sleep great for the first forty-eight hours when the body is adjusting to the lack of oxygen. While you will never be able to perform the same length phrases at high altitude as at sea level, you can get much closer after the body has adjusted to the lower levels of oxygen.

Reed players will experience changes in reeds. Again, when possible, forty-eight hours can make a big difference to both you and your reeds! Most double reed players will tell you to make the reed at the altitude that you are going to play it. Adjusting a finished reed generally is not very successful and, yes, this includes bassoon players. That said, there are reed-making techniques that help oboe reeds and can probably be applied to other reed instruments as well. First of all, I don't recommend changing everything. I know some use a wider shape at higher altitudes but that only causes intonation problems for me. Instead, I suggest a thicker gouge and a smaller diameter cane. On oboe, I use a gouge above 0.60, like 0.61 or 0.62, and 10–10.5 diameter cane.

In an article that I wrote for the International Double Reed Society, I discussed the measurements of reeds made at different altitudes and used a dial indicator to measure thicknesses of these reeds. After another twelve years living at seven thousand feet the measurements have remained unchanged, but I do have a few more observations. The biggest difference between the reeds of high and low altitude is overall length. My reeds are about a millimeter longer at seven thousand feet. Much of this comes from the length of the tip, which makes sense when you consider that there is less air to move so you need a longer tip to get things vibrating. I also found that the relationship of the spine to the back has more of a contrast. The back is thinner to a thicker spine.

You will also feel like you are doing more scraping if you are using the thicker gouged cane. While most of the thicknesses were the same, you have a thicker gouge so more scraping results. I find that the reeds I make at seven thousand feet look more integrated but have thicker rails going up the sides of the back, which stop at the heart. I always feel like I take a lot of cane off the sides of the tip and heart to get the reed to vibrate but measurements show that the end result is the same as on a low-altitude reed. In my measuring of thicknesses, I found that most of the thicknesses of the heart and tip were the same from altitude to sea level. I do have to change altitude often and seldom have forty-eight hours to make a reed once I get to a performance venue, so I keep reed boxes for different places at different altitudes. I can usually find a couple of good reeds to get by with for a day or two if I cannot make a new reed fast enough. I also take partially scraped reeds and finish them. This works better going from altitude to sea level, if you leave the reed heavy you usually can take more off at sea level. (You have to leave more cane on the reed in different places and make it longer if you are going up in altitude.)

Warning: If you have heart problems see your doctor before traveling to high altitudes especially if you also have trouble flying. I don't mean to scare anyone away, since the western United States has some of the most beautiful country that you will ever see and much of it is at high altitude. Most people have no trouble at all and those with asthma may find the clean air makes them feel better. If you do get out of breath—Stop! Remember that you cannot physically exert yourself the same way that you do at sea level, especially for the first forty-eight hours. One of my students' parents brings a small portable oxygen tank with her when she comes to Flagstaff, but most often if you feel funny, start drinking water. ➵

Fine-Tuning the Flute Section

Helen Ann Shanley

INGREDIENTS:
Tone
Pitch
Articulation
Vibrato use

SERVES:
The students, directors, listeners, and ultimately, the music.

Musical ensembles are mixtures of sounds and rhythms that combine in a variety of textures and timbres to serve to the listener. The flute section can be a brilliant color that is vibrant and tasty or it can be full of small problematic ingredients that detract from the final result. There are several qualities of the flute section sound that are often noticeable problems: lack of clear, ringing tone; poor intonation; improper use of vibrato; muddy or heavy articulation. All of these elements need to be addressed by the director in conjunction with the private teacher if he/she is fortunate to have a private lesson program. It is very confusing to the maturing student if the director and the teacher do not agree on the basics.

Tone
The tone color of a section depends, of course, on the tones of the individual players; however, the overall colors of the section should be firm and projecting for the lower register (not weak and hollow) and clear and full for the upper register (not shrill and forced). For most sections the tones will be immediately improved if: 1) supporting the tone is drilled as a constant element of playing; 2) the low register is strengthened by keeping the upper lip firmer with a more compact embouchure; and 3) the upper register is opened up more so that the aperture is larger and the jaw is more relaxed.

The individual problems students may have and their possible solutions are listed below:

Tone Sounds	Pitch	Possible Problems
thin and weak	flat	head-joint rolled in too far breath support is weak aperture too small and tight
thin and forced	flat/sharp	lips too flat against the teeth aperture too small and tight
windy, unfocused	sharp	flute is too high on the lip aperture is too spread

Tone Sounds	Pitch	Possible Problems
hollow, empty	sounds flat (but can actually be sharp)	aperture is too open air speed is too slow tongue is too low in the mouth
upper register shrill	sharp	jaw protrudes too far and is tense
lower register stuffy/closed	flat	air angle is too low head-joint rolled in too far

Pitch

Tone and pitch are very closely related, so many times if the tone is improved the pitch also improves. If the students consistently play "out of tone" and with poor pitch, always having to adjust their tone production to "fix" the pitch (e.g., playing with a small tone to avoid being too sharp) check to see if the head-joint could be lowered on the lip, which will generally lower the air direction, thus correcting both tone and pitch problems.

Another major intonation problem for the flute section is the pitch of extremes: playing too sharp in the high register or in a *forte* dynamic and too flat in the lower register or in *piano*. The *forte* dynamic level in any octave should have a lower air angle: jaw relaxed, more open; a *piano* dynamic in any register needs the jaw and lips more forward, maintaining fast air speed, raising the air angle. The students should always work to keep the tone focused and clear, regardless of dynamic level or register. Special attention should be paid to the alignment of the head-joint with the flute body: rolled in too far can bring about a flat pitch; rolled out too far raises the pitch. Most often a straight line with embouchure hole, keys and foot joint rod is the most satisfactory way to align the parts of the flute.

There are certain fingerings to help correct the most common problem notes:

Lower the pitch	Raise the pitch
E3: th-1-2 . . . 1-2 (no pinky)	E2: th-1-2-3 . . . 1-2 (2nd tr key)-pinky
F-sharp 3: th-1-3 . . . 2 (pinky)	F-sharp 3: th-1-3 . . . 3 (C/C-sharp keys) for soft entrances
A-flat 3: 2-3-G-sharp...2-3 (pinky)	
B3: th-1-3 . . . (both tr keys) 3 (pinky)	
C-sharp 2: add 1-2-3 right hand	

Have the flute students practice crescendo-diminuendo with the proper lip/jaw movement to maintain the pitch. They should also practice diminuendos keeping the air pressure firm, raising the air angle (jaw and lip forward). Using the air alone is not satisfactory; the players need to see the results on a tuning machine. Rolling the flute in and out is a "quick fix" but it disturbs the tone and the hand position.

One of the most important studies for the development of tone is the book *De la Sonorité* by Marcel Moyse (Leduc). This is an invaluable aid for the director to use as a techniques guide for embouchure development to aid in fluid movement throughout the registers, maintaining good pitch control.

Vibrato

Using vibrato in the flute section helps give a more vibrant color to the sound, but that technique should not take the place of a good, solidly supported tone. It is important for the flutes to be able to play with and without vibrato easily. The students should practice pulsing the tone (as in breath/rhythm/impulse) with a quarter note=60 at four beats, then five, then six. Varying the speed of vibrato helps the phrasing, using a faster speed for more musical intensity and a slower speed for a lyrical passage. It is necessary to be able to change the speed smoothly with a constant air stream. Be aware of the student whose vibrato is a "nanny-goat" sound that cannot be turned off: the throat is usually too tight (often from a lack of proper support). There are places where a well-supported straight tone is far better for the section: chorale passages with clarinets or the brass, and scale passages that can sound wobbly when played with vibrato.

Articulation

Articulation most frequently creates problems when 1) there is a difference in tone between the slurred and tongued passages, 2) when double tonguing is too short and choppy, or 3) when the student tries to make the tone work by tonguing too hard. For the first problem make sure the students keep the embouchure and vowel sound the same going from slurring to tonguing: often the embouchure becomes too loose and unfocused when articulating and/or the vowel sound changes from "tooh" to "tuh" or "tah." Frequently, the tongue moves too much in the mouth causing a heavy, "thuddy" sound, or the tongue moves back and forth, rather than up and down, thus distorting the tone.

The articulation written in flute parts of "slur two, tongue two" will sound much smoother and less bumpy if the students will practice connecting the last note of the slur to the first tongued note without clipping off the slur. This is exactly opposite from the replaced-tongue clarinet technique. Using this technique helps the air carry the line forward without so much separation and choppiness.

To correct the second problem, practice double-tonguing slowly in a legato manner: more tone, less tongue sound. The notes will be short enough through speed, not by clipping the notes abruptly. Use the syllables "tooh=cooh," connecting the notes with the air stream.

To smooth out the articulation (number 3) a note's response should not generally rely on tonguing: proper support and embouchure for that particular octave are the necessary elements. Remember, "Air makes the tone happen, the embouchure makes the color, and the tongue defines the beginning of the tone."

There are many etudes written by J.J. Andersen (Op. 15, 33, 41 various publishers) available for developing good articulation. The Karg-Elert Caprices, as well as the Donjon "Etudes de Salon" found in *The Modern Flutist* (Southern Music) are excellent for developing good style in articulation. Trevor Wye has a series of books available on different aspects of flute playing. Volume 3, *Practice Book* (Novello) is devoted totally to articulation.

Overpopulation

Many of the problems of the section develop from too many players and also from players who are not physically suited for the flute. It is extremely important for the welfare of the student and the group that only those who are capable of producing a tone clearly and easily should be put on the instrument.

When there are too many flute players then the director always has a hand up shushing the section, and the students therefore never really learn to play solidly and with good support. Often the director has the younger players either lay out or play passages down an octave to avoid high-register pitch/fingering problems. Changing the octave registration can accentuate the pitch problems and can also muddy the sonority.

Special Techniques for Developing a Good Section

Pitch control: Have the students play chords in the low and high registers, varying who plays the root, 3rd, 5th: to adjust the chord, raise the 5th, lower the 3rd. Always check the root with a tuner.

For greater smoothness and flexibility in wide skips have the students practice playing slurred harmonics with upper lip movement rather than just overblowing to achieve the upper partials. Teach them to play "Taps" fingering low C.

Teach them breath staccato to develop lifted releases and a light style of eighth-note staccato (more "tooh"). There is no release with the tongue ("tut") using this technique.

Admonish them to always play with wet lips.

Allow them to blow with a solidly supported air stream, but work hard on playing "piano" with a good tone, making it just a smaller version of a "forte" tone.

Keep reminding them that they have to learn to adjust the pitch quickly with the embouchure and jaw to match the instruments below them. They cannot just push buttons and tune out! Rehearse the flute lines with the bass parts in passages so that the players begin to learn to listen to others and adjust as they play. Directors can also rehearse the ensemble, changing the seating arrangement so that the instruments that play together often can hear each other better.

During marching season have as many flutists as possible play piccolo so that they become more at ease with the instrument. It helps lip flexibility to practice switching from flute to piccolo and back. The piccolo players should also work with a tuner so that they can learn to hear the correct pitches and know where to place the notes.

Have available a complete fingering resource book, such as James Pellerite's *A Modern Guide to Fingerings for the Flute* (Zalo).

Use the flute ensemble repertoire for development of stylistic techniques in the larger groups as well. Frequently these groups are left to fend for themselves because the students can usually play the notes. Details of playing are then often lost. ➞•

A Surefire Method for Transferring B-flat Soprano Clarinetists to the Low Clarinets

Richard Shanley

INGREDIENTS:
Select the right student. Selecting the "right student" is of primary importance. All too often a weak player with tone production problems or poor rhythm is moved over to an independent part in hopes that he can contribute more to the group than he did on 2nd or 3rd clarinet. This usually does not happen. Instead find a student who is eager to distinguish himself by playing a lower part, or switching when needed. The student should be able to make a full characteristic tone, independent rhythmically, and big enough to have good posture and reach the keys without hand or finger distortion.

SERVES:
All band and orchestra directors, private instructors, and clarinetists who wish to expand their performance horizons.

Why low clarinets?
In most public school ensembles the low reed sound is not as full as the low brass sound. Frequently good bassoonists with good instruments are in shorter supply than low brass players or clarinetists capable of contributing on the lower instruments. Granted, the orchestra must have bassoons but adding to or reinforcing the low clarinet sound in any musical ensemble (the band or clarinet choir in particular) will enhance the color of that group and produce a firmer bass on which to obtain better balance and pitch.

Experiment with low clarinets to obtain the best results.
There are myriad jokes about the alto clarinet, but altos are viable and useful in ensemble. Consider using them in ensemble only when they have an independent part, i.e. not when their part is doubled, particularly by another clarinet part. The bass clarinet is the most essential member of the low reed sound in band and contributes a unique color in the orchestra. Even in junior high school bands it is wise to double or triple the part. The contra clarinets are frequently overlooked at the junior high school, but even one E-flat contra-alto can give the ensemble a big boost. And, it is no problem to teach the student(s) to transpose tuba parts by simply imagining that the part is in treble clef and adding three sharps. For example, if the tuba part is in E-flat concert, then the E-flat contra would play in C. The BB-flat contra bass with extended range to low-C is usually an expense best spent at the high school and college level, and requires a great deal of care to ensure that the mechanism functions properly all the time. Composers frequently score the BB-flat contra bass too high.

Write out these parts for E-flat contra so that the BB-flat's higher part will be played in the stronger lower register of the E-flat contra. But when a low C is written, as in clarinet choir or Percy Grainger's band works, only the BB-flat contra will do the job.

Bass clarinets with extended range to low C are not required in most band music. But the quality of the extended instrument is sometimes worth the added expense and certainly does meet the demands of modern band and orchestra music. The BB-flat contra bass should only be purchased with the low C range in order to produce the lowest tones, much like a contra bassoon. All extended instruments have more mechanisms; therefore, they require greater care, especially when being assembled and disassembled. Some models of low-C basses can be purchased in one-piece cases. They reduce repair bills.

Use proper equipment.

It seems that the most common mistake is to select the wrong reed strength. Most are too hard for the low clarinet—so hard in fact that the low tones and articulations cannot speak with clarity. On most medium, medium-open mouthpieces (such as a Selmer C*) used on low clarinets, a number 3, 3.5, or 4 reed strength should be sufficient to match the mouthpiece facing. Note that alto clarinet mouthpieces, like Vandoren B44 or Selmer C*, usually require 2.5–3.0 strength reeds. Some performers prefer a slightly more open facing for the contras (Selmer C** or D).

The other common mistake is to use the wrong reed size on alto, and the contra clarinets. Most modern alto clarinet mouthpieces are made to use alto saxophone reeds. The E-flat contra uses E-flat contra or baritone saxophone reeds, while the BB-flat contra only uses reeds made expressly for that instrument. The ligature must hold the reed firmly on the mouthpiece or the player will experience undue warping at the point where the reed meets the facing and at the bottom of the windway.

The student must use a peg. The contras are fitted with them. If alto or basses do not have peg assemblies, install the model that can be soldered onto the bell rather than fitted on the body, where the wood may sustain damage. Use a neck strap to keep the student from cramping the left-hand first finger to stabilize the instrument. The alto or bass player may even try placing the tip of the peg inside of the right shoe for added security. Finally, the instrument must be in good working order so that the student does not have to squeeze keys to play. The most common problems, however, are those encountered with the "automatic" register keys. If these do not work properly, the student will not be able to play the full range of the instrument and may become discouraged and quit, thus compromising the entire transfer process and ultimately the low character of the band.

Identify similarities and differences between soprano and low clarinet embouchures.

In general the clarinet and low clarinet embouchures are very similar. In the initial transfer instructions it is usually best to tell the student to simply play the low instrument as if it were the soprano clarinet, and don't open up unduly and try to "play low." Instead, let the instrument do the work. The differences are dictated to a great extent by the instrument. Low clarinets require more mouthpiece/reed in the mouth. The mouth is wedged open to a greater degree by the larger mouthpiece. There is no need to pull the jaw back. The jaw is hinged. The more one opens the mouth, the more the lower jaw will pull farther and farther away from a tangent formed between the upper teeth and chin—but—the player will notice a need to simply pull the chin down rather than back, thus keeping the teeth more opposed. The corners of the mouth may seem even more puckered (without actually wrinkling the lower lip). The reed rests on top of the lower lip rather than against it, as in soprano playing. The tongue maintains its arch, achieved by saying "ooo" with the lips and " eee," "shshsh," "sheee," and similar sounds with the tongue, but not "oh" or "awh." The tongue is overall a bit lower in the mouth, not only to accommodate the larger mouthpiece, but also to facilitate the voicing of the lower instrument.

The angle of the instrument to the body is dictated by the shape of the low clarinet's neck. Irrespective of this, it is imperative to keep all low clarinet perpendicular to the player or with the bell drawn slightly closer to body. Do not allow the bell to push away from the body at an obtuse angle, as this promotes closing the reed against the mouthpiece. Establish the proper playing position with the head up rather than ducking it, as this too closes the reed and even the throat.

STEP-BY-STEP INSTRUCTIONS:
Two Ways to Determine the Proper Amount of Mouthpiece

1. Show the student that he must take more mouthpiece than in soprano playing. Illustrate this in two ways. First, drop a piece of paper between the reed and the mouthpiece. Scribe a line on the vamp of the reed where the paper meets the facing. Place your thumb on that mark and insert the mouthpiece in the student's mouth until the lower lip contacts the thumb.
2. Another way to guarantee that the student takes enough mouthpiece into the mouth is to have the student play an open G on the instrument, then take more and more mouthpiece until it squeaks, then back off just a sixteenth of an inch. Next draw a line against the teeth on the top of the mouthpiece and place a piece of electrician's tape on that line and tell the student to play with his teeth against the tape (not on top of it). These tricks work for all the lower instruments, but the teacher will notice that because of the more acute playing angle of the BB-flat contra, the amount of mouthpiece will not be significantly greater (if at all) than that of the E-flat contra.

The student is ready to play.

Start by playing a descending F major scale in the chalumeau register, because the use of the left thumb offers a bit more stability than other scales such as G major or B-flat major, which can be used later. Do not open up, or drop the tongue for the low notes. Simply increase the support to overcome the added resistance due to the longer instrument. Do this until a free, uniform tone is achieved. Next employ this tonal concept and physical feeling and play the ascending F major scale. Follow this by playing F–E, F–D, F–C, etc. to low F. Then begin on low F and play the passage ascending (F–G, F–A etc.). Next ask the student to play the above scales and intervals with diminuendos, then with slight spaces or eighth rests, and then with separate attacks. All of these attacks must be accomplished without jaw or embouchure movement! And finally, have the student play a simple bass line as in B-flat–F–B-flat–F–B-flat–F–G–A–B-flat first, slurred, then tongued lightly, then staccato, and finally with rests between each note. This will really reinforce the student's confidence and the ensemble's bass-line!

To achieve the clarion register, secure the proper voicing as in teaching the soprano clarinet. First employ diminuendo exercises from forte to piano on low-B-flat, A, G to low F or E. When a clear piano is achieved, lightly touch the register key while maintaining the wind pressure. Play clarion F, E, D, C, B-natural to gain confidence. Next start on low B-flat and work up to the thumb-F high-C twelfth. Next play the F or C major scale from top-line F to high C up and down to gain security. Do all of the same exercises prescribed for the lower register by starting on top-line F (rather than low B-flat).

At this point, the teacher may want to include a number of tonguing exercises in both registers to ensure that there is no throat or jaw movement while tonguing. The student may note that it requires a firmer tongue contact than in B-flat soprano playing to obtain clear tonguing in the lower register. The student may even feel that a bit more of the tip of the tongue contacts a bit more reed. This is especially true for larger downward skips into the lower chalumeau register where one has the feeling of almost immobilizing the reed before the fundamental can speak.

It is not immediately necessary to introduce the third register (altissimo). This register is not as difficult to produce as the clarion on bass or alto. But when the teacher decides to do so, teach it as you would on the B-flat soprano clarinet. Start with top-line F and simply maintain the "eee" tongue arch while executing a diminuendo and rolling the left-hand index finger downward to expose the half-hole on the first key in the left hand. Again, the diminuendo helps finesse, rather than force the note to speak.

Continue this process from F–D, F-sharp–D-sharp, etc. chromatically until the A-sharp–G interval is achieved. Play the chromatic scale from C-sharp or D up to G and down again. Once the chromatic is comfortable, practice the tonguing exercises prescribed for the clarion register. Note that the C-sharp can be played with the half-hole but some models of bass clarinets do not speak as well with the half-hole and actually require lifting the first-finger key. Almost all high Ds require the half-hole. Most all of the standard high Gs for B-flat soprano will speak on alto and bass. Don't be concerned with the third octave or notes above high C-sharp for the contra clarinets at this point in the student's development. There are a number of very useful, and in some cases better, "short" fingerings used by all professionals for the third octave on bass. But the fingerings and techniques above will allow the student to play the useful range of the instruments with relative ease in a very short time.

Cooking Time
Plan on just a couple days of good instruction to teach proper transfer techniques. A few more days will be needed to solidify these habits. The teacher will need to monitor the student's progress regularly until the student is secure with the instrument. And remember it is not a bad idea to let some students continue to play their B-flat soprano clarinet while also contributing on a low clarinet when needed. ➝●

Developing the Complete Woodwind Player

Kenneth Singleton

INGREDIENTS:

You start with a double woodwind quintet (two flutes, two oboes, two clarinets, two bassoons, two horns) of undergraduate students who have achieved a better-than-average level of development, plus a committed coach/conductor, a ready supply of great music, and a couple hours of rehearsal each week.

SERVES:

We all know that, even in the best of circumstances, there is often a chasm between one-on-one applied teaching and performance in a wind ensemble or orchestra. Chamber ensembles are often used to address this need, but there usually remains a noticeable gap. Working in ensembles of like instruments (flutes, clarinets, etc.) can certainly help students learn how to match and balance within the same family. Likewise, ensembles of different instruments encourage tuning, balancing, and matching articulations between diverse instruments (woodwind quintet, quartet, etc.).

Yet, when you stir these seemingly well-prepared musicians into large pot of players consisting of numbers of strings, brass, woodwinds, and percussion (better known as an orchestra; take out the strings and we'll call it a wind ensemble), most students are not at all prepared to take on the demands of upper level literature—especially the soloistic aspects.

The best medium I have found for teaching the essentials of ensemble playing is the double woodwind quintet (and the permutations you get when you add or subtract a player or two). There is great literature available for this medium, most of it from the classical and romantic eras. Within the ensemble, players must play soloistically, work in pairs of like instruments, and match pitch, articulation, balance, and style with numerous diverse combinations. A conductor may prove helpful, but in many situations is unnecessary.

I use the double woodwind quintet as a year-long ensemble "boot camp." Even though this is a rewarding ensemble for the most advanced players (is there *any* better music than the Mozart serenades?), I reserve it for freshmen and sophomores. (In addition, our wind ensemble performs much of this same music.) Participation is by invitation only, and students receive chamber music credit.

A performance is given each semester, but the ensemble mainly functions as a vehicle for teaching and learning. All aspects of ensemble playing are addressed, including tone quality, intonation, rhythm, articulation and note lengths, balance, pulse control, rhythm, musicality, stylistic awareness, formal analysis of the music, breathing, beginning pieces without a conductor, and, of course, being on time and ready to play at every rehearsal. Without a heavy performance schedule (first semester there are twelve two-hour rehearsals and 45 minutes of performed music), all these areas can (and must) be repeatedly addressed. Still, the impending performance keeps everyone focused.

I try to wean the students away from the conductor as soon as possible. It may be better to perform selected movements, rather than entire works, in order for students to develop the skills to play without a conductor. Likewise, the group may be split into several small chamber ensembles in addition to the larger group. A recent program featured selected movements from a J.C. Bach symphony (five players), a Dusek partita (three players), flute duets by Beethoven and Telemann, an octet by Krommer, plus double quintet pieces by Jacob and Spittal, none of which required a conductor. The programming for the spring semester usually focuses on complete larger works, for example Bernard's "Divertissement," Mozart's "Serenade No. 11," and Francaix's "Le Gay Paris" (with trumpet soloist—another underclassman).

Students who complete this "curriculum" are well prepared to play in orchestra, wind ensemble, or advanced chamber ensembles.

Ultimately, who does this serve? This recipe serves ten students, who take what they have learned (and are learning) from their studio teachers, and learn apply it to all aspects of ensemble playing. ➤●

A Clarinet Choir in Every Band? Improving the Quality of your Ensemble through a Real Choir Approach

Guido Six

INGREDIENTS:
Good ears
Team spirit

SERVES:
Bands and clarinetists.

Any instrumental choir has the disadvantage of being tonally limited to an ensemble of like instruments. Even when one has the entire clarinet family from the very low contra bass to the high E-flat or even A-flat sopranino, there are many tonal colors missing when compared to a full band or symphony orchestra. I suggest that directors should try to turn this disadvantage into an advantage. Is a band or orchestra not a collection of several instrumental choirs? Is it possible for a large ensemble to sound great when one or more of the instrumental choirs do not? I strongly believe that by developing good fundamental performance skills in single instrumental choirs, directors can significantly improve the quality of any larger multi-instrumental ensemble. The great challenge for a conductor in leading an instrumental choir is to accomplish more with less. Directors who can realize this with their instrumental choir will find it much easier to do the same with their larger group!

You only need one pair of good ears, a real team spirit, and a perfect balance.
When "Claribel" performed at DePaul University in 1994, people in the audience were curious about the equipment we were using. They seemed to be surprised that our musicians did not all play on the same instruments, same mouthpieces, same reeds, and same ligatures.

Although good equipment can do much to improve the quality of the sound, what really makes a difference is students learning to listen. Every player must listen through the same ears: the ears of the conductor who is responsible for developing the concept of sound he wants from the ensemble. Even if your students have the best equipment, if they are not playing correctly (with good embouchure, good breathing, good intonation, etc.) your instrumental choir will not have a good sound. When the priority of good playing fundamentals is coupled with students playing on superior equipment, then the ensemble has the best chance of realizing optimal results. Good players who are well trained in good playing fundamentals can sound acceptable playing on inferior equipment, however, players without good fundamentals will not sound good even when playing the best equipment available.

Just as with team sports, all members of an ensemble must commit themselves to making personal sacrifices for the benefit of the ensemble. In ensemble playing, there is no room for individual actions to take precedence. Everyone must know and accept his/her role in making the ensemble successful—if a musician cannot hear his/her neighbor there is something wrong (with either one or the other). If one can hear himself (loud and clear) at the expense of hearing others then there is also something wrong. All members must focus on the goal of playing with one unified sound. A director can help students achieve this within each part (i.e., first clarinet, second clarinet, etc.) as they learn to place their individual sounds within the overall ensemble unity of sound. These things do not happen separately, but rather they should occur together as students learn how to control their sounds according to the ears of conductor. Every voice must have a high-quality resonance that blends with the other "ingredients" in order to achieve the ultimate goal: the unique sound of your ensemble.

Using the right ingredients is very important; using the exact amount of each is even more important and brings us to the balance in the ensemble. Many clarinet choirs place too many players on the first part, put mostly the "weaker" players on the second and third parts, and have woefully few players on the alto and bass parts (which are the secret to stability and richness in the ensemble sound). If there is the possibility of having the proportionally correct numbers of all the instruments needed (no matter size your ensemble), a director must take care in making seating assignments for the musicians in the ensemble. As the conductor, you are blender of sorts. If you don't use the proper amount of each ingredient (each ingredient being a voice), the final result will not be as good as it might otherwise be.

Even when one has the correct balance of ingredients, conductors should be aware of the specific qualities that each ingredient provides. In "Claribel" the E-flat clarinet and contra bass clarinets are considered to be tonal seasonings. Just as a good chef is careful to use seasonings wisely, so must the conductor use tonal seasonings insightfully in creating the concept of sound s/he wants from the ensemble. These "seasoning" instruments should color the sound, not dominate the texture. Again, musicians must learn to use of one pair of ears (the conductor's!) in dishing out these tonal seasonings. Once this is achieved, you have the perfect tool to make the music more than notes and rhythms.

Every note is important, not every note is the most important.
I have heard many ensembles struggle to play with a well-defined homogenous sound where only the melody seemed to be of any importance. A melody will be even more beautiful when appropriately supported by the vertical aspect of music, the harmonic structure.

A good ensemble sound depends upon support from the lower and inner parts. The bass line should be like a cushion, providing comfort for the other parts to be spread upon, not unlike sheets and blankets on a bed. The more that is done to develop an ensemble's concept of sound from the bottom to the top, the more the listener (and player) will be at ease in performance. In "Claribel" we call it, "don't challenge the rules of gravity." Music is an outgrowth of natural principles. Why should the sound of your ensemble not conform to the principles of gravity?

When your musicians can hear each other and make a wonderful sound together, it is easy to help them understand the role of the other voices. In an ensemble that sounds good, one will hear every note that the composer has written. Important, yes, but is this the most important aspect of balance? By carefully studying scores in advance of rehearsal, conductors will be able to give insightful instructions to their musicians regarding the relative importance of their particular part at any given moment. By emphasizing the need to always be aware of how each part fits into the greater texture, the conductor will create an awareness in each musician of his or her role in bringing a piece of music to life. Making this a priority in your rehearsals from the beginning will save you time in future rehearsals, as your musicians learn to use their ears and make adjustments to more appropriately match their sound into the greater whole.

In creating a hierarchy of importance between melody and harmony, I believe it is important to look carefully at the alignment of the notes and their relation to the overriding harmonic structure. On a very simple level, music consists of notes either in the harmonic structure (chord tones) or notes not in the harmonic structure (non-chord tones). The former determines the harmony, the cadences, the key changes . . . (all things related to the vertical aspect of the music) while the second category is important in bringing out the expressive qualities contained in the melodic line and in other lines supporting the melody (the horizontal aspect of music). As music is constantly moving in time, the horizontal aspect (counterpoint) must be sustained within the vertical context (harmony) of the music. In this way, the conductor can capture the true essence of the music in a particular composition.

To help musicians become aware of the function of chord tones and non-chord tones, the conductor can choose a section in the music where the non-chord tones in the accompanying voices can be temporarily deleted. Playing the music once or twice in this way will help the musicians to hear the fundamental harmonic structure of the excerpt. After playing the passage without the non-chord tones, go back to the original composition. The conductor should explain the different non-chord tones (passing tone, escape tone, anticipation, suspension, etc.). Each of those "ornamental" notes has a different meaning and should be played in a way that brings out the natural effect contained in the construction of the music. Many ornamental notes are hidden in inner voices and do not receive the emphasis they need when the melody is allowed to predominate too much. Musicians playing the melody should realize that their part might not always be the most important. Particularly on sustained notes, the melody should pull back the volume a little bit to allow for the movement of the inner voices to be heard more easily.

Music is a language, the only language every human being can understand.

Music has a lot in common with spoken languages. Whereas spoken language delivers specific information or ideas, musical language contains the potential for emotional inspiration and revelation. I believe the emotional content of music is one of the most important aspects of our universal language, however, speaking to peoples' emotions can be risky. Therefore, it is important to teach musicians the grammar of the musical language in a way that enables them to use this knowledge to reach the listener on an emotional level. Understanding the function of non-chord tones as ornaments as well as properly delivering chord tones within the overall texture of the music is paramount. Knowing how to use musical punctuation is also very important. Composers typically try to make this as clear as possible in their music; however, sometimes this can be rather difficult to ascertain (for example, a good mystery writer does not give away on page 2 who is going to be murdered or who the murderer might be). Conductors have the responsibility to develop an interpretation through score study that is in agreement with the intensions of the composer.

In using music as language, composers are creating a story for us as musicians and listeners to experience. Sometimes it is easy for us to understand what is being represented (for example

Smetana's *Moldau*). However, other times we are challenged by an imaginary musical story with no script. In these situations, we as musicians should still try to be able to explain certain phrases, passages, and gestures by using our creative imaginations.

A final word to every musician in your ensemble: everyone in your instrumental choir is very important no matter what part they play. For example, a couple cannot get married unless they both say, "I do," or commit in some way to the relationship of the two as one. It is the same with all of the members of your ensemble. The conductor has the responsibility to nurture the commitment of each member in a way that endears all members to the musical bond necessary to produce a rewarding and enriching experience for all involved. I encourage you to lead your ensemble to a common musical cause through goodwill and your love for music.

Some of Claribel's golden rules:

You are as important as anybody else in the ensemble.

Anybody else in the ensemble is as important as you.

The ensemble is more important than the individual.

The conductor's input is limited to your commitment to rules 1–3.

Your commitment can push the conductor's input to perfection. ➤●

Warmed-Up Clarinet or How to Make Certain You Don't Just Have Leftovers!

Robert Spring

We, as clarinetists seldom think about the physical balance of our performance. The most important part of any day's practice time is the warm-up period. I have "cooked up" a comprehensive warm-up that I use daily in my teaching and playing. Each aspect of the warm-up leads from one to the next, and the objective is a warm-up of all muscle groups from large to small. The warm-up should emphasize relaxation and comfort with the instrument, and should cover all of the fundamental aspects of clarinet performance.

INGREDIENTS:
These include breathing, sound production, intonation, finger motion (both adjacent and nonadjacent), articulation (both single and multiple), registral sound unity, range extension, consistency, and combinations of the above.

SERVES
Clarinetists who care.

BAKING INSTRUCTIONS:
1. Begin with long tones. This, as well as the rest of the warm-up, is done with a metronome. Keeping things the same tempo everyday helps with overall consistency in performance. Play a chromatic scale in long tones. Set the metronome at 60 and play each note for four counts, breathing every four notes for four counts. This means that one is forced to exhale for 16 seconds without a breath. Make certain to breathe only in the rests, and try to maintain a solid *mf* sound throughout the range. Do this to make certain that every note on the clarinet is performed in a long tone fashion every day. I used fifths and twelfths for many years, but found this to be superior, as I was forced to listen to each note daily. Notes that had inferior sound quality or were not in tune with the rest of the clarinet were quickly fixed. Use a tuner to check the intonation on each note.
2. Next play the entire Klosé scale pattern (page 123 in most Klosé books) in either the melodic, harmonic, or natural minor form (vary these by day) at a tempo of quarter note = 60. Play the pattern slurred and expand each of these scales to three octaves when technique allows.
3. This is followed by page 14 from the Langenus Book 3, the major and minor arpeggios. These are also played at mm = 60 and are all slurred concentrating on smoothness. Every note should sound like the note in front of it and the note behind it!
4. Begin now to increase the tempo of the finger motion. Play the Klosé thirds at quarter note at 120, again all slurred. You do not want to introduce the tongue until the fingers

are relaxed and accurate. Increase the tempo again to 176 and play the Klosé scales in all three forms at 176, and the Klosé thirds and Langenus arpeggios at 160. If this tempo proves to be too rapid, perform at fastest clean tempo.

5. Now begin warm-up work on the tongue. Use page 22 from the Langenus Book 3, for single tongue warm-up. Dr. John Mohler (my teacher, now retired from the University of Michigan) stressed this exercise as being the single, most important for developing speed with the single tongue. The aspect of tension and release, tension on the two fast notes, and release on the longer note, is the same idea as tension and release that weightlifters and body builders use. I have found that during the twenty-five years that I have been working on this exercise my tongue speed and accuracy have gone beyond my wildest dreams. I begin at 120 and play the exercise four more times: 144, 176, 208, and 224. This is all single tongued.

6. Then introduce the single tongue with finger motion, again using the Klosé scales. Play them all tongued at 132 and two slurred and two tongued at 176. Again vary the minor form daily.

ADDED INGREDIENTS FOR SPICY PERFORMANCE

1. Warm up the double and triple tongue next. Play major scales using the pattern:

Play them at 120, 144, 176, 208, 240, and 288 if possible.

2. Follow this with scales triple tongued in the following pattern, two octaves and one note in range.

This is played at 160, 192, 224, 264, and 320 when possible.

3. Last do some circular breathing studies using again the Klosé scales pattern.

Baking Time

The entire warm-up takes about 45 minutes to 1 hour. Follow immediately with technical musical problems for the next 30 to 45 minutes following. As stated, everything in the warm-up leads one to the next, and every part of the clarinetist is warmed up. It seems to prevent some of the problems that many performers have with muscles, tendons, and other performer-related physical problems. This is very extensive, but I find that my students are not at a loss for technique when it's necessary. The long tones and slow playing help in sound stabilization, control, and endurance.

Serving Size and Special Needs

Do not vary the warm-up on performance days, do not warm up differently for different types of performances, and do not use a special warm-up for contemporary music.

I believe that we need to be teaching the comprehensive clarinetist and making our students aware that the physical aspects of performing the clarinet are every bit as demanding as those of the brass player. If I teach this to students, I find that they are "teaching themselves" so much more than if I do not insist on a comprehensive warm-up. After all, they are their own teachers most of the time. ➤●

Steve's Supersonic Seven-Step Saxophone Soufflé for High G—High Notes That Won't Let You Down

Steven Stusek

Even just a few years ago a saxophonist could get by with just the notes in the normal range of the saxophone. But today, most serious works for our instrument reach much higher. Although these notes used to be viewed as difficult to produce, saxophonists have been cooking long enough to have learned a thing or two about them. This recipe is for producing the first note in the extended range, high G—a note that is sure to be light, easy and delicious.

INGREDIENTS:
A good basic tone
Desire
Patience
Scotch tape

SERVES:
Serious saxophonists.

1. Whistle your favorite tune. Feel how your lips, tongue, cheeks, and air work together to change the notes of your tune? Playing high notes on the saxophone is very similar to this feeling (not exactly the same, to be sure). When we manipulate the tone on the saxophone with this synergy, we call it "voicing." "Voicing" is the key to playing high notes on the saxophone.

2. Because it is relatively easy to produce a tone throughout the entire normal range of the saxophone, many young saxophonists fail to make a solid connection between the feeling in their mouths, and the pitch that they produce. This first exercise is designed to connect ear, embouchure, and air. It creates the "voicing connection."

3. On the mouthpiece alone, play a concert A. Bend the pitch down a half step, and then return to A. When this becomes easy, try bending the pitch down a whole step, always returning to your starting A. As you gain control of this exercise, increase the intervals until you can bend the pitch down a P4 or greater. NOTE: You may be able to bend the pitch a half step by dropping the jaw alone, but still have difficulty bending the pitch further with this method. You need to connect the pitch, lips, tongue, cheeks, and air—in short, you need to learn to "voice" the notes. Don't be afraid to experiment at this stage! When you have mastered this step on the saxophone:

4. Reattach your mouthpiece to the saxophone and play high F with a good, solid tone (is there any other sort of tone?). Bend the pitch down a half step and return to F. As with the mouthpiece alone, keep increasing the interval as you gain control. Experienced

141

saxophonists can bend the pitch as much as an octave! To be sure, you can play some very high notes without being able to bend pitches as indicated above, but if you learn to "voice," the high notes will be very easy.

5. Here is the easiest fingering (among perhaps more than a dozen options!) for producing high G:

Octave key, B key, F key, side B-flat key, high F-sharp key. Saxophonists notate it something like this:

Finger this note on your saxophone, form your best embouchure (as always!), and try producing high G. If you blow like you do for the rest of the notes, you will more than likely produce a B-flat well below the G you want. You haven't made the "voicing connection" yet. There is only one thing you can do:

6. Grab your Scotch tape. The reason the G doesn't sound is that this fingering uses an acoustical phenomenon called "venting." In this case, the high F-sharp key/hole acts as a vent. Ideally, the vent hole should be very small, like an octave vent. The high F-sharp tone hole, however, is quite large, creating an unusual amount of resistance. We overcome this resistance by "voicing" a note. When we haven't yet made the voicing connection, we can "cheat" by making the hole smaller. Much smaller. Take a strip of Scotch tape (say 1.5 inches), open the high F-sharp key, and place the tape over the tone hole (sticky side against the tone hole itself), leaving perhaps a quarter to a third of the top of the hole *uncovered*. You can let the F-sharp key close on the tape (don't worry, the tape won't hurt your saxophone). In essence, we have created a small vent hole where there was a large one. Try producing the high G again—it should sing!

7. Of course, you will want to wean yourself off of Scotch tape. Play high G again (and again!). Bend the pitch, experiment with changing the shape of your mouth, vary how you blow into the mouthpiece (hey, now *this* is voicing!) until the tone is as clear and as beautiful as you could want it to be. Move the tape so that more of the tone hole, or "vent," is exposed, and play the note again, voicing it until it is again as beautiful as possible. (Did you notice how I slipped the word *voicing* into that sentence without quotations? You are already used to voicing!) Continue to move the tape so that less and less of the F-sharp tone hole is covered. Over a few days you should be able to play high G with this fingering alone. You will be Scotch tape–free, and on the road to playing all the high notes with ease.

NOTE: There are a number of excellent books on the market that contain exercises and fingerings for all the high notes on the saxophone. They include *High Tones* by Eugene Rousseau, *Voicings* by Donald Sinta, and *Top-Tones* by Sigurd Rascher. And these days one can easily find numerous fingerings on the Internet. ➙●

Saxophone Altissimo

Dale Underwood

INGREDIENTS:
A good instrument, a good reed, and patience!

SERVES:
Saxophonists who wish to play most modern repertoire.

The saxophone altissimo register has been used since the early decades of the twentieth century. It is the range above high F or F-sharp, depending upon the whether one's instrument has a high F-sharp key or not. In today's literature one needs at least one octave beyond the traditional palm-key notes, and to perform the Brant *Concerto* or the Ibert *Concertino da camera* in its original version, an octave and a fourth is necessary. Sigurd Rascher was the most famous of the pioneering saxophonists to perfect this register. His groundbreaking book *Top-Tones for the Saxophone* explains it quite well and provides great exercises to help along the way. In my opinion, the book *Voicings* by Donald Sinta and Denise Dabney is the most thorough book of our time on the subject.

The altissimo register is based upon the overtone series. This is produced by playing a low B-flat, and while retaining this fingering, playing all the notes in the series by changing throat position—in a sense, very similar to singing falsetto. First is the octave (B-flat), then the fifth (F), the second octave, (B-flat) third (D), fifth (F), seventh (A-flat), and the third octave (B-flat). Beyond the third octave, it goes pretty much scalewise. Another good exercise is to play a concert B on the mouthpiece alone, and then try and play a major scale down one octave. Then do intervals and arpeggios. Remember that usually when we start attempting these notes we have already progressed and developed some substantial skills.

Next, we start something new that doesn't sound all that well and frankly, can be demoralizing. Perhaps the major frustration is that the first note is usually G—the hardest of all altissimo notes because of the acoustical makeup of the instrument. There are many high notes that we can get at this point other than G. Some students get the G on the first try, while others take longer, and some really struggle with it. The common mistake is to only work on the G until we get it or get so frustrated that we give up. Normally we either get a G, or we overshoot and get a C-sharp. Stay with the C-sharp: it's a note we will need later!

Try to focus on the C-sharp (or whatever note we can get) and *work down* to the G. If we can get the G-sharp then it's a simple key movement from the side C fingering to the side B-flat and then we stand a good chance of obtaining the elusive G. A lot of it is confidence, knowing we can get these notes. I suggest not using vibrato and not trying to articulate at this point. Use breath attacks or slurs.

143

At this early point in the exploration of the altissimo, don't worry about intonation. Just get the notes—we can fix the intonation later. In a book written by the famous golfer Jack Nicholas, Nicholas states that when he was young his teacher taught him how to hit the ball as far as he could and not worry about were it went. He advised him to straighten it out later—all we want now is distance. The altissimo is much the same. Let's just get the notes now, and we'll get the intonation later. We need to have a solid note before we can adjust it.

Also, remember how difficult it was at first just to go over the break as a very young player. Lots of keys to move at the same time. Now we are using fingerings that are foreign to us. Many times, missing an interval is just a mater of not having the fingers coordinated. Work on the fingerings with just the horn but not playing. Commit the fingerings to memory so you don't have to rely on the fingering chart. And above all, make altissimo part of your daily practice! Don't work on it once or twice a week; do it every day! Some days it will be better than others. At first it will depend a lot on the reed but as you get stronger and more confident you'll be able to get it on almost any reed. ➞●

Reflections and Musings

Himie Voxman

INGREDIENTS:
A lifetime of contributions

SERVES:
Many generations of woodwind players.

The following are excerpts from my recorded conversations with Mr. Voxman, whose ninety-fifth birthday coincided with the last of these interviews. This article is a departure from the overall focus of this volume, included here to share a few thoughts of someone whose numerous contributions have touched us all. –CW

On Contributing to the Woodwind Literature

CW: I'd be curious to know how you met Mr. Gower. How did that relationship begin?

HV: At the end of each school year, Centerville's [Iowa] Music Supervisor would poll teachers of our grammar school graduates, which meant seventh and eighth grades in our case, for prospects for instrumental music study. That was not offered in our public schools at that time. She turned these names over to William Gower Sr., who was then the town band director for follow-ups. So Mr. Gower called my mother to see if she would like for me to have clarinet lessons. He had a hard rubber Albert System clarinet to sell for $35.00. She made a $10.00 deposit after asking me if I would like to study. I agreed to do so, although I must say, I never had any previous interest in music. The lessons began in June of 1925. So that's how I met him. Of course, from then on he was my teacher, for a few years at least.

CW: And then, when did you start collaborating on the methods?

HV: I have a diary from my junior and senior high school days, and I noticed that it was in 1928 I mentioned that we started talking about a method. I should explain that Gower wrote out the first twelve lessons for his own students—of his own compositions, so to speak—and then we went into Klose, and also I went into the Langenus method—which was a very good thing—at the same time. Gower was a trombonist, not a clarinetist; his great virtues were that he had a wonderful ear for quality of all the wind instruments, and for that matter, the violin. And he saw to it that I learned all the auxiliary fingerings out of the Langenus book. So that's more or less that connection.

CW: How about the Rubank connection? How did you get started with that?

HV: My earliest publication was an abridged version of Weber's *Recitative and Polacca*. The time I started teaching in Iowa City, my best high school student—I wasn't teaching in the school—this was private—my best high school student was Tom Ayres, who had just received a Division I rating in one of the mid-1930s national contests. I thought others might be interested in my abridgement, so I approached Rubank, and they accepted and published it, I think in 1937.

But back to the question about the methods, we put an elementary method together—we used Gower's six lessons—and then concocted the rest of it to make a school year's work. I think musically it probably had the best material of any elementary method at the time, and it moved rather rapidly. We were really thinking more of people who started in the seventh grade—in those days we didn't have that much school music, and people didn't start that early. And of course, the Rubank books were coming out at that time, and they were easier, but we took our methods to Jenkins Music Company in St. Louis—that was one of the largest music dealers. They looked at it and accepted it, and I think it did very well—I believe it sold 6,000 copies the first year. So I thought, well, it would be a good idea to follow up on that, so we started the *Advanced [Method]* book—I had done some work on it, and finished it. We took it back and I thought Jenkins would surely want that, but they were rather dilatory about accepting or not accepting it, so, having had some previous experience with Rubank, I took it there. And they looked at it, accepted it, and in the course asked for other books like it.

We first started talking about writing a method book in 1928. Our first book was called the *Modern Method for Clarinet*, and later, Jenkins didn't care to continue it. Of course it didn't sell much after the first few years. Charlie Eble took it shortly and reprinted—oh, I don't know—500 copies or so, disposed of that so he called it a day.

CW: So in 1928 when you started talking about this project you were still in high school?

HV: I wasn't out of high school yet—I started high school in '25. I was a senior, I think. I didn't do much with it until a few years later. The *Modern Method* didn't come out until '37, but by then I had done quite a bit on the clarinet advanced book—it has a copyright date of 1938, I believe.

CW: Let me go down a different avenue. How, as your career developed, did you get started adding to the literature—finding things to transcribe?

HV: How did I get started? Because I felt there was such a paucity of it. We all had a book, and that's as far as most kids ever know. They take the Rubank book or whatever . . . books before me . . . and it seemed to me that that was fine, but it seemed to me that that wasn't all there was to it. So I became, as I traveled over the country, I had opportunities—I always had great respect for librarians. Our librarian, Rita Benton, was internationally known. She did me a lot of good. She'd give me a little write-up—I could go to about anyplace—Frankfurt, Germany to the librarian, and have the person look at the little note and immediately I was accepted and I was permitted to go into the stacks. I was very fortunate in that regard. Rita Benton wrote two books on libraries of the world, describing their holdings, so if you wanted to go to Berlin you'd know what libraries to go to and so on.

CW: So in the process, if someone wanted to continue doing that sort of thing, the best avenue is still to get to know the librarians first?

HV: Yes. A lot of them can help you, and not only that, they know other libraries. When they see what your interests are, they can suggest where you ought to go, because they're familiar with other people's libraries. So I always had a very high regard for librarians and in my career I always felt that I owe a great deal to librarians all over the world.

On Style of Teaching

CW: Your teaching style—how do you think that developed?

HV: Well, of course, it's a little difficult to define style. You mention [in a letter sent prior to this interview] that when you played, I heard you through and made remarks afterward—I didn't stop you. I think I got that from different people. [Dr. Phillip Greeley] Clapp, by the way, speaking of influences—that's what he would do with the orchestra. We did a lot of sight-reading—we always sight-read a piece for many years, and he didn't stop. We'd finish, and go back and do it from there. I felt this way about teaching—I still do and maybe you do too—I like to hear a student go through a piece, and what's acceptable, that's fine, I'll approve of it, and what isn't acceptable, I'll tell him my notions of it. But I think it's important that they go through a whole piece. It's a little jarring for a student to go a few measures and be stopped, go a few more and be stopped—I think they get unnerved a bit.

CW: You know, when I get a student the first several lessons—very often it unnerves them *not* to be stopped all the time. Were you ever the kind of teacher that tore things apart measure by measure?

HV: No.

CW: Is that because of a philosophy about teaching, or is it just part of your personality? For example, with you I would get through a whole piece sometimes, with only one comment, whereas Mr. Marcellus would tear things apart measure-by-measure. Were you collecting things for that one or two wise comments, that I would carry with me all week long?

HV: I don't think you can just take a student and say, "You're a blank . . . we're going to start over." As much as you can, you ought to give the student credit—if he has some ideas—if you can find some—start there. I don't think it's right to make students feel uncomfortable.

I always enjoyed teaching, because in the first place you like to make contact with somebody else's brain, you know . . . at least I've always felt that way . . . and you have to do it different ways with different people. With a really bright kid you toss out a basic idea and figure, they're smart enough to expand on it. But there are others that say, here's no. 1, now I better give them no. 2. Some students want you to be so precise about what you say . . . and they'll go home and remember exactly what you said, but they won't expand on it and give them something to broaden. Sometimes they'll gladly accept what you told them but they don't realize that that's just the start. But I enjoy teaching, and you like to come in contact with somebody else's brain, and every student has a different one.

On Some of the Great Clarinet Pieces

CW: You told me a story one time about Stravinsky one time—something about the *Three Pieces* and a letter someone wrote?

HV: Well, it's rather an interesting story—I wish I could remember some phases of it. But what happened was, I had a doctoral student from Ohio and he had previously done some work on the *Three Pieces* and he asked me to hear it. He played in a rather free style—I say "free" in respect to rhythm. That is, the sixteenth didn't equal the sixteenth, and there were minor tempo changes here and there. I pointed out to him that Stravinsky indicated "sixteenth equals sixteenth" more than once and he meant it, but he continued to insist that since it was not accompanied, the performer ought to have some right to take some liberties. And rather jokingly I said, "Let's send him a letter and ask him about some places." And I drafted a letter—made it rather simple—I don't remember what I asked . . .

CW: You don't still have that letter then?

HV: No. I provided some blank lines at the end of each short question where he could write yes or no. And I don't know—for some reason I decided not to send it under my name—we sent it under the student's name. We were really surprised when very shortly we received an answer in red ink, with the yes's and no's indicated, in all cases very clear that the music was to be played as written, and the student did so after that.

CW: So there were yes's and no's, but basically he said, "Play it the way I wrote it."

HV: That's right. Unfortunately, the student left the university and I've never heard from him since. Needless to say, I very much regret that I didn't sign the letter [and retain a copy].

CW: Yeah—that would be a wonderful thing to have.

HV: Yes, it would. It's a little late now. ➤●

Flashy Fingers Flambé

Michael Webster

SERVES:
All woodwind players from a clarinetist's perspective.

In an article in *Clarinet* magazine of December 1999, I defined technique as being the physical attributes that allow effective conveyance of musical expression. That article, "The Architecture of Technique," stressed the many facets of instrumental mastery beyond playing fast notes accurately. To be a successful performer, those facets can't be ignored, but neither can brilliant finger technique. Any repertoire—recital, chamber music, or orchestral—will require controlled speed at one time or another.

INGREDIENTS:

First Ingredient: Posture
Fast finger technique begins with the feet! Shinichi Suzuki (1898-1998) knew this and gave each young violin student a personalized cardboard foot stencil on which to stand during the earliest lessons. A firm, well-grounded stance helps to align the spine and facilitate the development of neural pathways through the arms to the fingers. When we practice finger technique, we are training small muscles, to be sure, but more importantly we are training the neurological system—that fascinating and complex labyrinth of nerves that connects the brain to all body parts via the spine. We all know that a severe spinal injury can cause paralysis, whereas a healthy spine serves as an efficient conduit through which signals can pass, unimpeded, from the brain to the fingers.

The nerves consist of a series of fibers separated by spaces called synapses. Every time the brain sends a signal to a finger a synapse is bridged, and through repetition the nerve fibers achieve quicker and more efficient communication. Ultimately the nerves fire so quickly that the thought "C major arpeggio" achieves a rapid result without a specific, separate thought for each note.

Good posture enhances neural development. Start by grounding your feet well. Practice distributing weight from heel to toe and inside to outside until you reach a comfortable balance. Then stack your body on top of your feet by adding 10 percent more weight toward the heels, tilting the pelvis alternately forward and back until you achieve a comfortable neutrality in the lumbar curve (the curve in the small of your back). Raise your sternum (breastbone), place your head over your shoulders, and surrender the shoulders and arms to the gentle pull of gravity. This alignment of posture seems easy, but requires daily reminding and a certain kind of relaxed effort. In general, most of us will find that the sternum wants to sag, the head wants to be forward of the shoulders, which in turn want to roll forward or shrug. Once good posture is established you are ready to hold your instrument, with the nervous system eager to respond to instruction from the brain.

You may be asking, "What if I sit when I play?" Sitting is required for some instruments, such as the bassoon, and in some situations, such as when playing orchestral or chamber music. In that case, your grounding comes from the ischial tuberosities (commonly called the sit bones) that protrude from the bottom of the pelvis on either side. They form the base for stacking the body when sitting. While sitting, it is much easier to lose the lumbar curve by slouching. Ideally the chair must be flat or tilted slightly forward, and also must be the appropriate height for each individual player. The knees should not be higher than the pelvis, so taller people may need to seek a higher chair, use a firm pillow, or thin bolster, or—as a last resort—cross ankles underneath the chair. Make it a lifelong habit to monitor posture daily!

Second Ingredient: Efficient Hand Position

Hand position varies subtly from player to player and not so subtly from instrument to instrument. For example, the flutist's left index finger is very curved so that the bottom of the finger near the knuckle acts as a balance point, supporting the instrument. By comparison, the ring finger and pinky are less curved. Clarinetists must develop a downward angle of both index fingers, with gentle curve at each knuckle, and bassoonists must spread their fingers wider and straighter.

Individual differences range from the obvious (differences in hand size and finger breadth) to the less obvious (varying knuckle strengths, including double jointedness), to the least obvious (relative finger lengths). As an example, the index and ring fingers can be equal in length or one can be longer than the other. Because the left hand of the flutist and both hands of the clarinetist require index fingers to be more curved than the ring finger, it is an advantage for the index finger to be shorter than the ring finger. Don't despair if this isn't the case! Just be aware that relative finger length affects finger position. A clarinetist with long index fingers may have to overlap the ring with the fingertip more than other players, for example.

Third Ingredient: Economy of Motion

Regardless of hand position dictated by instrument and individual physiology, basic finger motion should come from the third knuckle, where the finger attaches to the hand. Starting with fingers in the "down" position, lift them one by one, keeping the same shape in the "up" position so that each finger moves as a unit from the third knuckle. Avoid allowing the fingers to become straighter or more curved as they lift. Think of having two home bases. Down base is easy: it is dictated by the holes, rings, and keys of the instrument. Up base is more challenging: the fingers must be trained to keep the same shape as in down base, stopping quickly one-half to three-quarters of an inch above the instrument. Practicing fast passages at a slow tempo but with lightning-fast travel between bases is a very efficient way to develop flashy fingers.

The exception is when a finger is required to manipulate more than one key. The clarinet has two excellent examples. The right pinky must travel among four keys on two levels. If a player were to try keeping the same shape from the upper to the lower level, she or he would have to draw the whole hand away from the instrument, greatly compromising speed. Rather, the finger needs to curve less for the upper level and more for the lower level without allowing the first or second knuckle to collapse. The index finger of the left hand needs to find three distinct levels: most curved on the tone hole, less curved on the A key, straightest on the

G-sharp key. The challenge is to minimize the amount of change from one level to another for fastest negotiation of rapid passages.

Fourth Ingredient: Controlled Relaxation
It is good to be relaxed, but if you are totally relaxed you are asleep! Take inventory of the work that must be done to play a woodwind instrument. The sternocleidomastoid muscles raise the sternum; the abdominal and intercostal muscles supply air; the facial muscles form the embouchure; the arms support and the fingers manipulate the instrument. For greatest efficiency the fingers must be relaxed but firm, sealing the holes well without pressing too hard. Use the following exercise to achieve optimum "touch."

The grace note must be as short as possible and also very clear and distinct. It is an exercise in speed. How fast can the finger go "down, up" or "up, down?" How firm and controlled can it be, while remaining relaxed? The finger motions should have two characteristics: lightness of touch and closeness to the instrument. The shortness of the grace note guarantees lightness for "down, up" and closeness for "up, down," so concentrate on staying close for "down, up" and light for "up, down."

The dotted rhythm should be very precise. A true sixteenth note will feel long after having played grace notes. A partner playing constant sixteenths or a subdividing metronome is very helpful. Retain lightness and closeness during the moving sixteenths and test your finger control by tonguing one repeated note and reversing direction seamlessly. This rhythmic sequence is also very valuable in coordinating two or more fingers, especially if contrary motion is involved. For example, B-flat to D-flat in the low register of the clarinet requires lifting the right index finger while dropping the left pinky. Practicing the rhythmic sequence with each finger separately and then together is a very efficient way to encourage positive, automatic neurological development.

Fifth Ingredient: Smart Practicing
All of the analysis in the world is useless without intelligent practicing, and lots of it! Follow the three "Ps" of practicing: persistence, patience, and playfulness. The need for persistence is obvious, but often our impatience causes us to try attaining a goal too quickly. The process is as important as the product, so be sure to take care of the goose if you want more golden eggs. Have you ever said to anyone, "I work the flute (or oboe, clarinet, or bassoon)?!" Of course practicing is work, but we must remember to "play" our instruments and retain a childlike joy when facing a page filled with quick notes that need to be learned in a short amount of time.

Here are some strategies for practicing a string of fast notes:
1. Play the passage several times, giving an even pulse for each note at a tempo wherein you cannot possibly make a mistake.

2. Extract short groups of three to five notes and practice them repetitively, gradually gaining speed. Three notes can be thought of as two pickups and a downbeat, with the pickups evolving into grace notes as speed increases.

3. Link two or more of these short groups. Two groups of four notes could be "short, short, short, long; short, short, short long." The long note is held until the brain recovers and effectively commands the next group with control and accuracy. Never allow the fingers to get ahead of the brain. It is often effective to place the long note on the most difficult note of the passage.

4. Gradually add notes to the fast group. For example, master the first three notes of the passage, then four, then five, etc. Or choose the last note of the passage and gradually add notes before it. Or choose a difficult note and gradually add notes before it.

5. It is okay to make a mistake! In the words of conductor and motivational speaker Ben Zander, smile, throw up your arms (without dropping your instrument!), and say, "How fascinating!" Then return playfully to the project at hand. But—**Do not repeat mistakes!** Choose note groupings in which you are quite confident of success, "auralize" (imagine the sound of) what you are about to play, and if your fingers don't meet your expectation, immediately alter the groupings by playing fewer notes or slowing the tempo. Repeated mistakes train the neurological system to make mistakes!

6. Don't forget your embouchure and air supply! Different notes have different degrees of resistance, especially when changing registers. It is quite possible for the fingers to work well, but for the passage to be marred by a note not speaking due to lack of embouchure focus or appropriate air supply.

Final Ingredient: Fire!

If Weber writes "Allegro con fuoco" or Schumann writes "Rasch und mit Feuer," we are being told to "play with fire!" Our parents cautioned us against that, but as musicians we must learn to create an impression of wild abandon when the music calls for it. If the fingers have been well coached, they can be counted upon to do their job at any speed, while we give significant attention to the air, which adds drama by shaping virtuoso passages with crescendos, diminuendos, accents, sforzandos, and subito piano or forte.

Fast fingers plus inventive use of the air equals fire, and your audiences will always appreciate having been served Crêpes Suzette or Bananas Foster rather than plain vanilla ice cream. ➤●

How to Play Well with Others

John Weigand

INGREDIENTS:
Proper preparation, a functional ear, and a working brain

SERVES:
Everyone in the ensemble and the audience.

Preparation:

It is absolutely essential that every musician is totally prepared for every rehearsal and performance. Playing the correct notes with perfect rhythmic accuracy is a prerequisite to being a good ensemble musician. Colleagues quickly lose respect for players who make mistakes in rehearsals or concerts.

Balance:

Below are general guidelines for how loud to play in a particular context. Ensemble playing is a very fluid situation, so this is just a good starting place.

When playing in harmony, the 1st-chair player (melodic line) leads, and the 2nd player (harmonic line) plays at the same dynamic. (1:1 ratio)

When playing in unison, the 1st player should be stronger, and the 2nd player should usually play somewhat less. The ratio can vary depending on the circumstances. In loud dynamics the players may be almost equal in volume, and in soft dynamics the ratio may become 4:1. This enables the 2nd player to easily tune to the 1st player, and the result will be two players sounding like one.

When playing in octaves, the 2nd player (lower octave) should lead, with the 1st player (upper octave) playing about half as loud (1:2 ratio). Since the 2nd player is playing the lower octave at a louder dynamic, the 1st player should tune to the lower octave played by the 2nd player.

These guidelines also apply when two different instruments play together (oboe and bassoon, for example).

Leadership:

It is the responsibility of the section leader to establish the standard of performance and musicianship for the section. It is the responsibility of the 2nd player (and other section players) to match that standard, and make their playing conform to that of the section leader. The 1st player must play with consistency to enable the 2nd player to match, and should notify the 2nd player in advance of any changes.

Intonation:

It is very important that every player be able to play their own instrument in tune, and is aware of the general pitch tendencies of their instrument as well as any problems with individual notes.

Lower instruments must establish the root of the chord accurately and securely. Higher instruments playing the root should match the pitch of these lower instruments.

Instruments playing the 5th of the chord should listen to the root and form a perfect interval with that pitch.

Instruments playing the 3rd of the chord should place their pitch according to the effect desired. For a feeling of stability and resolution (for example the last chord of a piece), major 3rds should be lowered and minor 3rds should be raised until the interval sounds "pure." For a feeling of tension or motion, the 3rds can be placed according to equal temperament, resulting in a mild dissonance.

It is critically important for the musician to develop a good sense of relative pitch, which will allow for adjustment of intonation "on the fly." There are many factors that can affect intonation in a performance situation (room temperature, reeds, etc.), requiring that every player listen constantly and make the necessary adjustments. Learn to anticipate intonation problems on your instrument, and make adjustments in advance.

Occasionally bringing a tuner to a rehearsal to resolve a particular problem is acceptable, but there are players who put their note in a particular place according to the device, thereby absolving themselves of any responsibility for intonation problems. These players are very insecure and should spend more time improving their listening skills and leave the tuner at home. Above all else, there is no substitute for tuning by ear.

Listening tips:

The traditional seating of the wind section of a symphony orchestra is not an accident. Almost everyone you need to listen to for intonation is seated behind you. You can hear them much better than they can hear you.

Give 'em a break:

Be aware of those around you, and help them, if possible. For example, when a flutist is in the low register, be aware that it is difficult for them to play very loud or short. If an oboist is playing in the extreme low register, it is difficult for them to play very softly. Be a good ensemble player, and adjust your dynamic or note length to help them. If another musician has a particularly difficult trill, don't play your easy trill as fast as possible. If you are playing a pitch that others need to tune to, be sure you are well in tune, but above all, be consistent, so they will find your pitch in the same place every time.

Respond to the conductor:

When a conductor (or your section leader) asks you to play something differently (louder, shorter, etc.), make a noticeable change in your playing the very next time. Look for other similar passages and make the same changes. Don't be stubborn and resistant to change.

The basics:

It goes without saying that every musician is expected to show up for every service on time and ready to play his or her best. It should not matter what kind of a mood you are in, and all your reed work and instrument adjusting should be done outside of rehearsal.

The result:
You will become a well-respected professional musician. Your colleagues will welcome you into their ensemble, and will likely be glad to return many of the same favors you are giving to them. ➼

Good Manners (of Articulation) Are Essential

Mark O. Weiger

INGREDIENTS:

Articulations in music are the equivalent of pronunciation in language and thereby can affect meaning. It is the difference between Cor Anglais (English horn) and Cor anglé (angled horn), or even Cor Anglaise. In art, articulations could readily be equated with the idea of working with only primary colors versus working with the entire Crayola box. Oboist Marcel Tabuteau, who for many years served as the principal oboe with the Philadelphia Orchestra, made remarkable strides working with all wind players in areas of phrase and sound balance. His instructional recording is still available and can be found in many libraries. Stevens Hewitt, a more recent former member with the Philadelphia Orchestra, went the next step when devising his marvelous method book. Within this method, one topic he introduces is the identification of several articulation styles.

SERVES:

All wind instruments.

If you agree that there are indeed a variety of articulation styles available that will bring woodwind players to a more united and homogenous state, then consider further that with this variety comes more interesting stylistic mannerisms in performance. Consider also the greater lexicon with which to express the different periods, mediums, and genres of music. But how does one go about employing anything other than the long, the short, and the accented so uniformly enforced in our secondary schools and community programs?

With phrases such as "attack" or "hit the note on the head" or "staccato means short" being bantered about in texts and rehearsals, woodwind players learn to associate the tongue as being an initiator of these concepts. However, as these are indeed *wind* instruments being played, it is the wind that is the true initiator, whereas the tongue is merely the tool that allows the wind to escape into the instrument or that which holds the wind back. In other words, the tongue regulates the flow of air through the reed or mouthpiece. The tongue then, acting as a door, controls how much air is to pass and how often. It is *the duration of this event that will determine the manner of articulation.*

Keeping in mind that this is not the sort thing one learns through a correspondence course, the following nine basic articulation styles with explanations are drawn from standard articulation markings found in music of all styles, genres, and periods. The most valuable articulation will be the legato. The term *legato* means connected. It will first be necessary to learn to play a truly legato-connected scale before adding articulations onto it.

Legato: All will recognize this as the "slurred scale." The slur sign has to do with air. To help make it truly connected, push the air across the notes, past the fingers. Think glissando between the notes, throughout the scale. To do this it may be useful to use the "gooey fingers" approach so that every note has a glissando connection to avoid any bumps or pops along the road. The "gooey fingers" approach involves moving one finger at a time as slowly as possible to generate a true, full gliss between two notes. Aim to get as much of a glissando as possible without any skips or jumps. It will require a great deal of control and relaxed manner so employ patience. This will be especially useful for any cross-fingerings or multiple finger movements between notes. A true legato is never as easy as it sounds.

Ex. 1 Legato   **Ex. 2 Tenuto legato**

Tenuto legato: This is a legato with the most delicate tongue stroke. The idea here is to generate a series of tongued notes that is as long and as connected as possible. For a string player this would mean using a *portamento* style on the same bow. For wind players it will mean maintaining the same air to connect the line. For reed players, the tongue should only lightly tongue the reed with a "D" rather than the usual "T" stroke. Focus will be on the front of the note for the "D" stroke but aim to avoid any decay of air at the back of the note.

Tenuto: The slur has been removed but the degree of connection will still be strong. The same "D" stroke is in play, with the biggest difference being at the back of the note. Here there will indeed be some decay of air. Some might consider having the smallest degree of separation in the manner of block tones. However, the word *tenuto* means held not separated. Consequently, it is not the degree of separation but the degree of decay that is the focus. Using the metronome set at a slow tempo you can best determine how late to begin the decay. In the decay process the close of the note should not be complete, but be more of a "dew-dew-dew" effect.

Ex. 3 Tenuto   **Ex. 4 Leggiero legato**

Leggiero legato: Here the slur is back, but the tenuto dashes have been changed to dots. The connection is still strong and the "D" articulation stroke is still in play. Unlike the *tenuto legato*, the focus will not be at the front of the note but at the back of the note. These notes will have a lilt or bounce to them and will have still greater decay than the tenuto notes. The speed of the tongue in making the "D" stroke should be faster than that of the preceding *tenuto leggiero* and the *tenuto*. In the decay process the close of the note could nearly be an "N" with the full syllable effect being something of a "don-don-don."

Leggiero staccato: This will be more toward the usual or ordinary articulation style and marking. There is neither a slur nor any dots or dashes employed. With this articulation marking it is always advisable to consider the mood or the context of the music and the genre and period. For slower works that employ this marking, it is generally accepted to use longer, more connected articulation strokes, whereas in faster movements, a lighter articulation might normally be employed. In early works that are unedited, it is common to consider adding articulations based on the mood and context presented. In some cases it is a good idea to borrow articulations from the work as a whole where no markings are used. However, in this case, this articulation style will be the median point in this series of articulation styles. As such, it may either employ a "D" stroke or a "T" stroke at the front of the note. The amount of decay at the back of the note will be greater still than the *leggiero legato*.

Ex. 5 Leggiero staccato   **Ex. 6 Staccato**

Staccato: Meaning separated or detached, staccato can have many gradations. The use of staccato within an *adagio*-style movement is such an example. Normally the staccato notation in such a movement would not necessarily be performed as short notes, but as notes with some degree of separation. While focus will be on the closure of each note, this can be done using the air (the "bah" articulation stroke) or with the tongue. Many are greatly offended by the so-called stopped-tongue approach to different staccato articulation styles. However, with practice the stopped-tongue approach can be quite gracefully executed and will ultimately provide still far greater varieties of articulation. Learning to close off a note with tongue will come when the choice of syllable ("tut") is adapted to more a "don" effect. Know that it is the length of note that provides the basis for the different articulations.

Martellato: This will require a heavy tongue articulation at the front of the note and with a fair degree of separation between the notes. It is also known as the hammer stroke, in which the hammerhead hits the nail without a recoil. Others call it the stopped-bell stroke, thus affording something slightly more graceful and less Sousa-like.

Ex. 7 Martellato   **Ex. 8 Tongued Accent**

Tongued accent: This is another form of the hammer stroke but one in which the hammerhead hits the nail and recoils. Each note should generate a pinging quality with the separation of each note being less than that generated by the *martellato* stroke.

Wind accent: This uses just the wind and no tongue. Some use a laughing gesture or puffs of air to generate the effect. While it is rarely seen, it can be found in some works of Mendelssohn and Sibelius as well as some chamber works such as the often-played Barthe *Passacaille* for quintet. It is most commonly notated like a tongued accent but under a slur. Most wind players see this notation and simply make it a tongued accent. For string players it would have an entirely different meaning, such as using the same bow stroke but adding weight at each change of note. For some it is an indication to employ a vibrato accent or so-called left hand accent. Not every accent in every piece should be treated equally. Again, the context, genre, and style of the period should always be taken into consideration.

Giving exception to the wind accent, it is generally assumed that all of the aforementioned articulation styles are generated using the tip of the tongue. Some individuals have found the term "tip of the tongue" to be too vague. It is possible to *think* you are using the tip of your tongue to start the note but in fact are using just under or just above the true tip. It is possible and useful for some to experiment with just what part of the tongue was in fact being employed. Some may find it useful to even experiment with using a part of the tongue further back from the tip. Certainly there exist other articulation styles that function for our instruments and that surface in different idioms.

Once you have discharged this mission with your usual messianic zeal, try using them to match your colleagues in quintet, band, or orchestra. It should open up a whole new world for ensemble playing. You might consider doing challenges within your ensembles as to who can master all of the articulation styles most effectively. Keep in mind that scales are merely the practice approach. It will become a greater challenge still, to use it as a performance practice.

While it is true that addressing the issue of articulation is a small beginning, you must agree that this small beginning can quickly lead to bigger deeds. It has been said that the more you learn, the less you have to practice. So start learning and start sharing. ➤●

Intonation Hors d'Oeuvres

Charles West

INGREDIENTS:
Ears that can recognize the difference between good and bad intonation
A desire to conquer the intonation quirks of the woodwinds
The ability to teach intonation in a structured way

SERVES:
Conductors who prefer that their ensembles play "in tune."
Musicians who like to play "in tune."
The listening public.

Knowledge and understanding are the tools that differentiate between satisfactory results and superior results. This article is an hors d'oeuvre tray filled with fairly random morsels that will help us to close that gap between satisfactory and superior intonation across the woodwind section.

Hors d'oeuvres for everyone:

- Dynamic change affects flutes and double reeds the opposite of single reeds. At soft dynamics, double reeds flatten somewhat and flutes may flatten a great deal. Single reeds, on the other hand, go sharper as they get softer.
- The attack on a single reed instrument is always slightly sharp and then drops to playing pitch about a second later, because the gas being blown into the instrument initially is more oxygen-laden than later on, when it contains higher levels of carbon dioxide. You can prove that gas density affects pitch by blowing a small amount of helium into any wind instrument: the very light gas allows the reed to vibrate more quickly, pushing the pitch remarkably high in the same manner as it affects the human voice. Carbon dioxide, after the tidal air (from the mouth, trachea, and bronchi), that never reached the alveoli in the lungs is denser than the air initially inhaled, slowing the reed and slightly dropping the pitch. (People who drink carbonated soft drinks while practicing occasionally experience this phenomenon to the extreme, very much by accident!)
- The attack on flute tends to be flat and then rise to pitch because the air speed tends to be lower at the point of attack then increases after the tone is established. Though gas density affects the flute as well as single reeds, the influence on the pitch (to sharpen) is overwhelmed by the change in airspeed.
- The pitch level on all wind instruments rises as the instrument warms and drops as it cools.

- Dirt in tone holes flattens the pitch emitting from that hole. Dirt in a register key flattens the upper register.
- Some instruments have more fingerings for each note than others. Until one reaches the altissimo register, the saxophone has the simplest fingering chart of all. While this might seem at first to be an advantage, it eliminates the possibility of choosing a different fingering to adjust the intonation of a particular note. Clarinet and bassoon, on the other hand, are rich in fingering options, each with its own pitch, color, and response characteristics. An intonation problem might be easily remedied by picking a different fingering, such that no embouchure gymnastics are necessary. Interestingly, a somewhat smaller smorgasbord of fingerings is also available for oboe and flute, but players tend to have firm ideas about whether more than one fingering is even necessary. There is much information in this volume about fingerings on bassoon (Hammel), and there is a volume of information by Cooper and Toplansky. Other books exist by Ridenour (clarinet), and Pellerite (flute) that explain fingering options in detail much greater than can be found in this volume.
- Electronic tuners are useful, but only to a point. In reality, we can find a better placement of pitches within a chord if we understand which member of the chord we are playing and how it needs to be altered to be more "in tune." Equal temperament, which is what the piano and the electronic tuner uses, by its very nature spreads "out-of-tuneness" (the Pythagorean Comma) over the twelve semitones so that it is less noticeable. Virtually all educated ears are pleased to hear the major 3rd of a triad played as much as 14 cents flat, or the minor 3rd of a triad played as much as 16 cents sharp. This deviation becomes even more extreme in the case of the seventh of a dominant seventh chord, which sounds best as much as 31 cents flat! To play in this way is called "just intonation," and it gives us a result vastly more satisfying than equal temperament.
- The second reality about real musicians as opposed to electronic tuners is that high instruments sound better slightly sharp and low instruments sound best slightly flat. Tuning a compound octave with piccolo and a bass clarinet by ear will result in the piccolo being sharp to the electronic tuner. What is actually sharp is what we hear as "in tune!" Know when to put the electronic tuner away!
- Finally, remember that the notes that emit from the tone holes closer to the place where the instrument is "pulled out" will be flattened more by the "pull" than those farther down the instrument. Thus, open C-sharp on saxophone or open G on clarinet will be much more severely affected than notes that have more fingers down. The whole scale changes when an adjustment is made.

Hors d'oeuvres for flutists:
- Flutists particularly need to know what to listen for. Flute teachers commonly emphasize from day 1 that the tone must be pure—free of excess "airiness." The educated ear will forgive an "airy" sound that produces the correct pitch much more readily than it will accept a pure tone that is flat! Young flutists often roll the flute in too far as a result of focusing on what a flute sound is *not* rather than what it *is*. By thinking "not airy," they discover that by rolling inward, "airiness" goes away—unfortunately the pitch goes flat. The rule of thumb is that one third of the blowhole is covered by the lower lip in the lower register, with somewhat more coverage in the middle, and yet more in the upper register. Be sure students' arms are not draped over the back of their chairs, causing their flutes to roll inward. Also be sure that they are not "ducking" their heads to get low notes.

161

- The head joint cork affects the intonation of the flute within itself, just as the baffle of a clarinet mouthpiece affects the clarinet scale. The conventional wisdom is that the line on the cleaning rod belongs directly in the center of the blowhole. However, many flutists find that setting the line very slightly to the left of center (up the flute) brings a more acceptable result tonally as well as more acceptable intonation.

Hors d'oeuvres for oboists:
- Reeds must be scraped with some semblance of the "American style"—a defined tip, heart, spine, windows, or back. Store-bought reeds are often mass manufactured and do not have these characteristics. Stable intonation is almost impossible.
- Ideal total reed length is 68 to 71 millimeters. Longer will be flat, requiring biting and improper embouchure to bring up the pitch, and shorter may be sharp. Additionally, the tone quality will be compromised and the reed will be uncomfortable to play.
- The reed should be pushed into the well of the oboe as far as it will go for appropriate intonation. (This is a common problem with beginner oboists.) Cork grease or sandpaper as necessary are possibilities, though compressing the cork on the tube by rolling it under a reed knife or table knife generally works better, preserving the cork and keeping grease off of the reed itself. Pulling the reed out of the instrument up to 1 mm is acceptable to lower pitch. However, any more will destabilize the entire scale.
- The height of certain keys can affect the pitch of individual notes. Adjustments can be made by a specialized oboe repairman. High C-sharp is especially flexible, and its pitch is easily raised or lowered by turning the set screw on the left hand first finger (half-hole) key on all but the least expensive oboes.
- Taking too much reed into the mouth causes the pitch to be sharp and the tone to be bright and unfocused, especially on fourth-space C. Be sure you can see some of the wood of the reed outside the student's mouth.

Hors d'oeuvres for clarinetists:
- An extreme pull at the barrel may cause throat tones (the pitches E through B-flat between the chalumeau and clarion registers, written on the lowest three lines of the staff) to be flat in relationship to the longer fingerings like the B or C immediately above the break. For this reason, it is best to tune the open G first, lowering the pitch by pulling between the barrel and upper joint. Once open G has been established, tune the C above it (sometimes called "tuning note C"), lowering this pitch by pulling the lower joint from the upper—between the two hands. If middle-line B is sharp, one could pull at the bell, but remember that since low E is flat on most clarinets, pulling at the bell would make the low E even flatter.
- Barrel joints vary widely—the most obvious variable is its length, though variations of interior diameter and degree of taper also influence the instrument's tuning as well. In the broadest sense, increasing the barrel diameter makes the twelfths larger. Thus, a clarinet whose clarion register (from middle-line B to C above the staff) is sharp in relation to the lower register will be helped by a barrel with a narrower diameter, and one whose clarion register is flat will be helped by a wider barrel.
- Mouthpieces also affect tuning, not only by placing the overall pitch of the instrument higher or lower, but by compressing or stretching the scale in each register. When the mouthpiece chamber (the open space under the reed) is larger, the short fingerings can be flat to the longer fingerings. Sometimes, people who work on

mouthpieces will change the baffle (the back of the chamber) to change the tone quality, and the intonation of the mouthpiece will then be affected.

- The short story on barrels and mouthpieces is, ALWAYS take a tuner with you when you buy a barrel or a mouthpiece. Many people have fallen in love with the sound, only to find out after playing either for a while that it is just too difficult to play in tune in the ensemble. Remember however, that a mouthpiece that negatively affects one instrument may positively affect another. TAKE A TUNER!

Hors d'oeuvres for bassoonists:

- See Bruce Hammel's recipe, earlier in this volume.

Hors d'oeuvres for saxophonists:

- Like all wind instruments, the saxophone has its bad notes. Fourth-line D, for example, is always sharp, just as half-hole F-sharp on bassoon, third-line B on clarinet, and so on—it's an acoustical property of the longest overblown fingering. However, improper embouchure makes things much worse. A correct embouchure should produce concert A-natural on the alto mouthpiece alone. Often students who play badly out of tune are producing a pitch much higher, even up to concert C or C-sharp.
- The good news is, the saxophone is a very flexible instrument. If the embouchure is working correctly, one can take advantage of the instrument's ability to bend upward and downward to place pitches in just the right spot! Be sure you produce a concert A-natural on the alto mouthpiece alone to be sure the embouchure is working correctly. ➤●

Other books in the Meredith Music Cookbook series

THE MUSIC DIRECTOR'S COOKBOOK
Creative Recipes for a Successful Program

Mark Aidrich
Kenneth Amis
Terry Austin
Frank L. Battisti
Jay Bocook
Peter Loel Boonshaft
Lynn M. Brinckmeyer
Michael Burch-Pesses
Charles F. Campbell, Jr.
John E. Casagrande
Rebar Clark
Jim Cochran
Michael Colgrass
Gary Corcoran
Paula A. Crider
Thomas C. Duffy
Cheryl Floyd
Richard Floyd
Eileen Fraedrich
Rob Franzblau
David C. Fullmer
David R. Gillingham
Steven Grimo
Alan Gumm
Frederick Harris, Jr.
Samuel R. Hazo
Leslie W. Hicken
Roy C. Holder
Shelley Jagow
William Jastrow
Barry E. Kopetz
Kenneth Laudermilch
Tim Lautzenheiser
Edward S. Lisk
Mitchell Lutch
Matthew McInturf
Allan McMurray
Charles Menghini
Stephen W. Miles
Linda R. Moorhouse
Willis M. Rapp
Jeffrey Renshaw
Nathalie Robinson
Timothy Salzman
Deborah Sheldon
Thomas E. Slabaugh, II
Frederick Speck
Lawrence Stoffel
Carl Strommen
James Swearingen
John A. Thomson
Johnnie Vinson
Barry Ward
Renee Westlako
Garwood Whaley
Carol Zeisler
Dennis Zeisler

THE BRASS PLAYER'S COOKBOOK
Creative Recipes for a Successful Performance

Jeff Adams
Kenneth Amis
Roger Bobo
Lisa Bontrager
Velvet Brown
John Clark
Dale Clevenger
Abbie Conant
Jeffrey Curnow
Kurt Dupuis
Peter Ellefson
Laurie Frink
Jack Gale
Wycliffe Gordon
James Gourlay
Toby Hanks
Dick Hansen
Kevin Hayward
Lesley Howie
Gregory Hustis
Alex Iles
Ingrid Jensen
Dave Kirk
Craig Knox
Mark H. Lawrence
John Marcellus
Raymond Mase
Steven Mead
Brad Michel
Gregory Miller
Bob Montgomery
Jennifer Montone
Daniel Perantoni
Marc Reese
Ronald Romm
Mike Roylance
Jon Sass
Ralph Sauer
Susan Slaughter
Phyllis Stork
Deanna Swoboda
David Taylor
Kenneth Thompkins
Demondrae Thurman
Richard Todd
Adam Unsworth
Warren Vache
Tom Varner
William VerMeulen
Charles Vernon
John Wallace
Froydis Ree Wekre
David Werden
Jeremy West
Gail M. Williams
R. Douglas Wright
Douglas Yeo

THE STRING TEACHER'S COOKBOOK
Creative Recipes for a Successful Program

Gilda Barston
Susan E. Basalik
Louis Bergonzi
Jeffrey S. Bishop
Muriel Bodley
Judy Weigert Bossuat
Ffirni Butler
Tanya Lesinsky Carey
Christina Castelli
Lisa Cridge
Winifred W. Crock
Patricia D'Ercole
Andrew H. Dabczynski
Sandra Dackow
Jean Dexter
Anne Donnellan
Ian Edlund
Teri Einfeldt
Gerald Fischbach
Kathy L. Frishburn
John Fitchuk
Jesus E. Florido
Robert Gardner
Jan Garverick
Beth Gilbert
Robert Gillespie
Midori Gotо
Karin Hendricks
Georgia Hornbacker
Kathleen A. Horvath
James Kjelland
Dottie Ladman
Scott D. Laird
Lori Lauff
Denise Martz
Joanne May
Peter Miller
Steve Muise
Debra K. Myers
Martin Norgaard
Ray Ostwald
Judy Palac
Bob Phillips
Jack Ranney
Donald Schleicher
Laurie Scott
Phillip W. Serna
Peter Slowik
David W. Sogin
David Tasgal
Laura Mulligan Thomas
Gwendoline Thornblade
Stephanie Trachtenberg
Mike Trowbridge
Kristin Turner
Mary Wagner

THE CHORAL DIRECTOR'S COOKBOOK
Insights and Inspired Recipes for Beginners and Experts

Hilary Apfelstadt
Ronald Boender
Geoffrey Boers
Lynn Brinckmeyer
Paul Broomhead
David L. Brunner
Simon Carrington
David M. Childs
Ann C. Clements
John M. Cooksey
Edith A. Copley
Lynn A. Corbin
R. Paul Crabb
James F. Daugherty
Steven M. Demorest
Rollo A. Dilworth
Dwayne Dunn
Mon Edmundson
Kevin Fenton
Janet Galván
Mary Goetze
Stephanie Bartik Graber
Alan J. Gumm
Paul D. Head
Michael D. Huff
Eric A. Johnson
Michael Jothen
Mary Kennedy
Henry Leck
Diane Loomer
Alan McClung
Joe Miller
Nina Nash-Robertson
Weston Noble
Granville M. Oldham, Jr.
Christopher W. Peterson
Rebecca Reames
Dave Riley
James Rodde
Kathleen Rodde
Catherine Roma
Paris Rutherford
Joanne Rutkowski
Pearl Shangkuan
Vijay Singh
Rick Stamer
Z. Randall Stroope
Barbara M. Tagg
Axel Theimer
Edgar Thompson
Robert Ward
Guy B. Webb
Susan Williamson
Judith Willoughby
Tom Wine
John Yarrington
Steven M. Zielke

The Music Director's Cookbook:
Creative Recipes for a Successful Program
ISBN 1-57463-039-3 $24.95

The Brass Player's Cookbook:
Creative Recipes for a Successful Performance
ISBN 1-57463-075-X $24.95

The String Teacher's Cookbook:
Creative Recipes for a Successful Program
ISBN 978-1-57463-091-6 $24.95

The Choral Director's Cookbook:
Insights and Inspired Recipes for Beginners and Experts
ISBN 1-57463-078-4 $24.95

Notes

Notes

Notes